Differential
Social Program
Evaluation

Differential Social Program Evaluation

Tony Tripodi
Phillip Fellin
Irwin Epstein
The University of Michigan

F. E. PEACOCK PUBLISHERS, INC.
ITASCA, ILLINOIS 60143

To FEDELE F. FAURI

CONTENTS

LIST OF TABLES

PREFACE

Since the publication of our book, *Social Program Evaluation* (F. E. Peacock, 1971), there has been a proliferation of texts and readers on program evaluation. Yet there continues to be a deficit of materials aimed directly at administrators who primarily use, rather than conduct, evaluations.

This book is a refinement and an elaboration of *Social Program Evaluation.* The change in title is meant to reflect the further development of the theme of differential evaluation, not to suggest that this is an entirely new book.

In it we continue to emphasize the importance of administrative involvement in planning for evaluations. We have updated and revised all of the chapters from *Social Program Evaluation,* striving to maintain technical accuracy; and we have added bibliographies for each of the chapters. Toward this end, we have benefited from reviews in the social science and social work literature, as well as from the comments of students, program directors, and program evaluators.

The single most important emphasis in this book is that of differential evaluation, which is essentially devoted to matching evaluation strategies to program stages of development, in accordance with the criteria of efforts, effectiveness, and efficiency. Hence, we include a chapter that has the purpose of clarifying the concept of differential evaluation and that suggests the kinds of evaluation questions that can be answered by a variety of different strategies.

Tony Tripodi
Phillip Fellin
Irwin Epstein

Chapter One

AN INTRODUCTION

THE DEMAND FOR EVALUATION

In the past decade, administrators and program planners have given considerable attention to the modification of existing health, education, and welfare programs and to the development of new programs to meet the needs of selected segments of the population. More recently, there have been budget cuts for many social programs by sponsors who have been increasingly concerned about the extent to which programs have satisfactorily delivered services or promoted social change.

As more attention has been focused on the public responsibility of social programs, demands for evaluation have increased. Program directors are being asked by funding sources, professional groups, clientele, and a more sophisticated general public to demonstrate not only the needs to which their programs are addressed, but also the contributions they make in solving or alleviating social problems. In addition, questions about the management of funds and the relative costs and efficiency of alternative programs are constantly being raised. For the administrator, the availability, appropriateness, and adequacy of program evaluation can determine the success and/or survival of a program.

Despite the increasing demand for evaluation from outside sources, administrators are often skeptical about the merits of program evaluation. Frequently they are confused by the claims and counterclaims of evaluation consultants representing different schools of organizational analysis. Moreover, some program directors view evaluation cynically, simply as a device used by agency supporters to justify current operations. Alternatively, in the hands of program critics, evaluation is viewed as a justification for reductions in program funding. In addition, legislators and clients alike have questioned the costs of evaluation—the former in terms of the lack of success in providing significant feedback of information to programs, and the latter in terms of the direct services these funds might otherwise provide.

THE PURPOSE OF THIS BOOK

Although administrators are frequently perplexed by decision-making problems concerning evaluation, most books on evaluation are written for evaluators. These books are concerned with logical and practical procedures in the conduct of evaluation studies. Often they include sections pertaining to the administrative context in which evaluation takes place and discussions of potential barriers to evaluation that emanate from conflict between program and evaluation personnel. But, typically, little attention is devoted to the problems of administrators or program directors in deciding when and what kind of evaluation is needed and how to use the results for making programmatic decisions. For example, in the recent two-volume *Handbook of Evaluation Research,* edited by Marcia Guttentag and Elmer Struening, there is virtually no conceptualization of social programs and the types of tasks and decisions made by administrators and their staffs. Consequently, the administrator who searches the literature is likely to find that it is of little use in making the kinds of evaluation decisions he or she has to make.

This book is written primarily for practicing administrators and program directors in the fields of health, education, and welfare. In addition, it may be used as a supplementary text by students of administration, program development, evaluation, and research in fields such as social work, public health, education, public administration, and sociology.

Our basic purposes are to provide a framework for making decisions about social program evaluations and to increase the sensitivity of program directors to different issues in evaluation. More specifically, our aim is to present guidelines that can be used by program directors so they can be more knowledgeable about raising appropriate evaluation questions and can make the best use of evaluation consultants.

Directors of health, education, and welfare programs are committed to improving societal conditions through their programs. Accordingly, they have important and difficult responsibilities to maintain. They are accountable to significant and diverse community groups, and, more specifically, they are responsible for reporting on program operations and achievements to intended program beneficiaries, program sponsors, program staff, and the general public.

In addition to their many responsibilities, social program administrators must frequently contend with pressures from a variety of sources. In many instances, they must make quick decisions in ambiguous situations and with little systematic information for guidance. Although it is not possible for all decisions to be made on strictly rational grounds, we assume that program directors prefer to base decisions about their programs on available, objective information in order to provide the most effective and efficient services possible within the scope of their programs. Moreover, with increasing demands for evaluation, program directors are not always in a position to make decisions about whether an evaluation should be conducted. Often, evaluations are demanded by funding agencies or by pressure groups outside the program. But even in those situations, the program director is in a position to influence the conduct and use of an evaluation. The more sophistication the program director has about evaluation, the more likely it is that the director can play a role in increasing the relevance of an evaluation of his or her program. Furthermore, the program director is often the primary consumer of evaluation studies and, as an effective administrator, *should* play a major role in planning evaluations of his or her program.

There are substantive differences among health, education, and welfare programs, but there are also many similarities involved in the administration and evaluation of such programs. Consequently, we attempt to stress similar problems of evaluation for these different types of social programs. A major emphasis is on differential evaluation, that is, different kinds of evaluation questions and techniques geared to different stages of program development. But the central thesis of this book is that evaluation is a management technique for the systematic feedback of information to be used to improve social programs.

SOCIAL PROGRAMS AND SOCIAL PROGRAM EVALUATION

Social Programs

Social programs are conceived broadly as having the goals of providing health, education, or welfare services for the advancement of individual or social change. Programs vary in dimensions such as the range and complexity of objectives, staff size and diversity, administrative structure, length of time in operation, operating expenditures, sources of support, and physical location. One program may include the entire range of objectives within a particular agency, such as the Office of Economic Opportunity's (OEO) community-action programs. Another program might include only a limited segment of an agency's activities, such as the use of nonprofessionals as public-health aides in a neighborhood health clinic. Established programs as well as developing programs are considered social programs. Thus, all of the following may be considered social programs: the total operations of a public-welfare department; the activities of a welfare-rights organization; an effort to deliver chest X-ray services to a rural poor group; inoculation programs for influenza; reading tutorials; and the entire activities of a public-school system.

Although the content of social programs and the means for achieving their goals may be different, all programs have similar problems to solve. Among these problems are location of resources, allocation of funds, maintenance of operating budgets, submission of reports to interested groups, and the justification of decisions regarding program planning and development. Moreover, social programs go through roughly similar stages in the process of program development.

Stages of Program Development

Program development may be described as a process with three sequential and interrelated stages: program initiation, program contact, and program implementation.[1] *Program initiation* refers to that stage in which the ideas for a program are translated into a plan of action and in which necessary resources are secured. It involves all of the planning and preparation required before the content of the program can be delivered to its recipients. In this initial stage of development, program directors are concerned primarily with the procurement or selection of material resources, staff, technology, and clientele.

Program contact is that stage in which a program has achieved its objectives of initiation and is devoting its efforts to the active engagement of a target population with the program staff. The program focuses on providing relevant program content to its designated clientele. In this stage of development, program directors are concerned with locating physical, social, and psychological obstacles to the effective delivery of services; locating other community resources that will aid, or impede, or substitute for the program's own activities; and so forth.

Program implementation is that stage in which a program, having achieved the necessary conditions of initiation and program contact, applies its technology, services, and so on toward the attainment of ultimate program goals. Here, the program director is concerned with the extent to which major organizational goals are achieved. In this stage, criteria for follow-up activities and possible program termination are specified.

---

[1] A similar conception of program development can be found in Jerald Hage and Michael Aiken, *Social Change in Complex Organizations* (New York: Random House, 1970).

Although these stages overlap somewhat, they are useful for specifying the conditions necessary for successful operation at different points in program development. In chapter 2 we examine program development in detail and illustrate program requisites within the different stages of development for a variety of health, education, and welfare programs. Moreover, in that chapter we provide guidelines so a program director can determine in which stage(s) of development his or her program is.

Social Program Evaluation

Planning for social program evaluation depends to a great extent on specifying program requisites within the different stages of development. This is necessary so both evaluators and consumers of evaluation know what is to be evaluated. In addition to the delineation of program requisites and goals, there likewise must be a clear specification of the proposed evaluation and its objectives. Program administrators and professional evaluators may have different conceptions of evaluation, and the failure to articulate such differences may result in inadequate planning for evaluation studies. For example, some differences appear to arise from varying uses of the word "scientific." What is scientific, objective, and value-free for one person may be nonscientific, subjective, and value-laden for another. Among evaluators, for example, Edward Suchman[2] used the word scientific to

[2] Edward A. Suchman, *Evaluative Research: Principles and Practice in Public Service and Social Action Programs* (New York: Russell Sage Foundation, 1967).

refer to the incorporation of experimental and control groups in evaluative research; Samuel Hayes[3] discussed the art of evaluation and implied that scientific refers to the obtaining of objective, systematic, and comprehensive evidence related to program activities; Clarence Sherwood[4] broadened the definition of evaluation to include strategies and skills other than those of social research; and Howard Davis and Susan Salasin[5] indicated that evaluation should include consultation regarding social change.

Another potential source of variation in conceptions of evaluation pertains to differing emphases on one or more of the following dimensions of evaluation: program efforts, program effectiveness, and program efficiency. Evaluation of *program efforts* refers to the description of the type and quantity of program activities. Evaluation of *program effectiveness* is concerned with whether intended outcomes, and beneficial unintended consequences, have been attained as a result of program efforts; and evaluation of *program efficiency* is devoted to determining the relative cost of achieving these outcomes.

Throughout the book we regard social program evaluation as a device for the feedback of program information to program directors and to other persons responsible for the continual development of social

---

[3] Samuel P. Hayes, Jr., *Evaluating Development Projects,* 2nd ed., reprinted (Belgium: UNESCO, 1967).

[4] Clarence C. Sherwood, "Issues in Measuring Results of Social Action Programs," *Welfare in Review* 5, no. 7 (1967): 13–17.

[5] Howard R. Davis and Susan E. Salasin, "The Utilization of Evaluation," in *Handbook of Evaluation Research,* vol. 1, eds. Elmer L. Struening and Marcia Guttentag (Beverly Hills, Calif.: Sage Publications, 1975), pp. 621–66.

programs. More precisely, *social program evaluation is the systematic accumulation of facts for providing information about the achievement of program requisites and goals relative to efforts, effectiveness, and efficiency within any stage of program development. The facts of evaluation may be obtained through a variety of strategies, and they are incorporated into some designated system of values for making decisions about social programs.*

Basic to our conception of social program evaluation is the idea of differential evaluation. *Differential evaluation* is a process of asking different evaluation questions of program efforts, effectiveness, and efficiency for each program stage of development and then choosing those evaluation strategies that are most appropriate to the evaluation objectives. In chapter 3 we present a range of different kinds of evaluation objectives for health, education, and welfare programs; in chapter 4 selected evaluation strategies are presented and discussed to provide the administrator with some information about their use. Included among the strategies are *monitoring strategies,* such as the administrative audit and social accounting, *cost-analytic strategies,* and *social-research strategies.*

Throughout this book we emphasize that evaluation is not synonymous with formalized research strategies, and that different evaluation strategies are more or less appropriate for providing information to accomplish different evaluation objectives. Thus, the administrative audit may be most appropriate for evaluating program efforts during the program-initiation stage, and a combination of experimental and survey methods may be most appropriate for evaluating program effectiveness during program implementation. To explicate this idea further, chapter 5 includes a matching of evaluation questions and evaluation strategies for different stages of program development.

Social program evaluation provides facts relevant to a determination of the achievement of program goals, but these facts may be interpreted differently. Although there are varying degrees of objectivity in the compilation of facts for an evaluation, the conduct and interpretation of evaluations is imbedded in a set of values regarding program goals and the "social good." Essentially, a *value* is a stated opinion of what is or is not desirable, and it is possible that individual values and societal values may be discrepant. For example, a program devoted to increasing the occupational skills of high school students may cause program participants to drop out of school to obtain a job. Those dropouts may be regarded as failures by school authorities but as successes by the program staff.

Another example pertains to welfare recipients. On the one hand, welfare mothers who receive welfare payments may be regarded by some persons as failures if they receive those payments for more than a stipulated period. On the other hand, it might be argued that those welfare mothers may be providing necessary care and supervision for their children, and if they do this well the program might be construed as successful. In a public-health program that involves the dissemination of birth-control devices, a reduction in the birth rate for a particular ethnic group may be regarded as desirable by some persons, but the intended "beneficiaries" may view the reduction of their birth rate as undesirable, since it may be regarded as an attempt to lower their dignity and self-respect. Hence, the same facts, irrespective of the objectivity maintained in securing them, could be construed as indicative of program success or failure.

PROGRAM DIRECTORS AND EVALUATION

Pressures on Program Directors

There are various pressures on social program directors for evaluation. There may be *mandatory* evaluations requested by funding groups, boards of directors, or higher administrative authorities. These evaluation requests may take forms such as progress reports on the accomplishments and failures of the program and reports that demonstrate the program management is responsible regarding its accounting procedures and its allocations of funds. The program director must comply with those requests, for they are from groups to which he or she is directly accountable. If the program director does not respond to such requests, he or she may either argue that an evaluation is not needed or risk the possibility of not receiving continued support for the program. Particularly with developing programs, which may be funded for a short period by such sponsors as the federal government, the program director may be caught in a conflict between program needs and the pressure for evaluation from the funding agency. In addition to these pressures, there may be few funds available for the conduct of evaluation, and the group that requests evaluation may not know, itself, what information it wants. Thus, the program director may be confronted with the dilemma of deciding what kind of evaluation, at what cost, is sufficient.

Some mandatory evaluations are conducted and funded by persons not directly involved with the social programs. In those instances, the program director may believe that he or she is one of the objects of evaluation and fear that his or her job is in jeopardy. Hence, the program director may be reluctant to participate in the evaluation and may be suspicious of the evaluation effort.

Pressures for evaluation may also arise from social and political groups that may be directly or indirectly involved with the social program. Charges regarding alleged discriminatory practices, program inequities, and mismanagement of funds may be made, with the possible result that an investigation of program practices is initiated. Difficult or impossible demands may be made on a program director; yet his competence is brought into question if he is unable to respond with factual information that he has accumulated about the program. Thus, external demands may compel the program director to call for an internal evaluation, that is, self-evaluation, of his program.

The pressure for *internal evaluation* may arise from the

program director and his or her staff, with the primary purpose of improving the program. For example, there may be a perceived lack of success of the program, or it may be felt that there should be some reallocation of program activities. On the other hand, the pressures may arise from the professions to which the program administration and staff belong; they may believe that they are obligated to provide a quantity and quality of services that are in keeping with current professional standards.

The Role of the Program Director

Because of a variety of pressures, and perhaps skepticism regarding the purposes of evaluation, program directors may believe they have minor roles to play in the planning of evaluation. Program directors are often preoccupied with finding ways to get the most from their budgets, trying to obtain resources for improving the operations of the program, and attempting to keep good financial records. At the same time, program directors must be aware of the activities of the personnel who are operating the program and keep up with their public-relations and public-information obligations. When a mandatory evaluation is called for, a program director may be reluctant to devote much staff time and energy to it. He or she may not want to divert funds from maintaining program operations to the evaluation and may even view evaluation as a device that can be used only for the purpose of justifying cuts in the program's operating expenses.

In spite of the above difficulties, program directors can play a key role in the planning of social program evaluations. Indeed, if the notion of evaluation as a management tool is accepted, program directors have a primary responsibility to plan for evaluations of their programs. Furthermore, from a practical point of view, the more the program director knows about his program from evaluation, the more able he is to improve the program and to respond to the demands for evaluation from groups to which he is accountable.

A program director does not need to be an expert in conducting program evaluations to participate meaningfully in planning for program evaluation. But what does a program director need to know to contribute to the process of planning for an evaluation? The program director should have some conception of different kinds of evaluation and the dilemmas of evaluation with which he or she is confronted and should have sufficient skills to know when to use evaluation consultants for evaluating different stages of program development. In connection with the above, we specify in chapter 6 the major dilemmas of evaluation that confront administrators of social programs: evaluation at what cost, what kind of evaluation, evaluation by whom, and evaluation for whom. In addition, several guidelines that might be useful in making decisions to resolve those dilemmas are presented. Moreover, in chapter 6 we specify ways in which the program director can use evaluation consultants more effectively.

THE SOCIOPOLITICAL CONTEXT
OF EVALUATION

Social Relationships in Evaluation

The process of evaluation involves obtaining systematic information within a context of social relationships. Persons who have vested interests in the planning and the results of an evaluation may represent different ideologies and value systems. Therefore, a crucial element in obtaining useful evaluations is the extent to which the key persons involved in evaluation are able to make appropriate accommodations to each other. Useful evaluations are more likely to occur when these conditions are met:

1. There is a clarification of the purpose of the evaluation among the key persons involved.
2. There is an agreed-upon commitment, contractual or understood, regarding the uses and possible consequences of the evaluation.

The key persons who may participate in the planning and the use of evaluation studies are the evaluator and his or her staff, the program director and his or her staff, persons with fiduciary responsibility for the program (such as sponsors and higher level management), and potential consumers who have no direct fiduciary or operating responsibilities regarding the program. Of course, the persons who participate in evaluation vary from program to program, and the number and diversity of persons involved depend upon factors such as the size and complexity of the program being evaluated.

Evaluations are initiated most frequently by program sponsors, separate from or in conjunction with program management. Often an evaluation consultant is sought, and the planning for evaluation is done by the consultant, who elicits cooperation from program administration and staff. In the conduct of an evaluation there is interaction primarily among the evaluation staff, program staff, and program administration. The key persons who participate in the use of results are those closest to the decision-making power, that is, the program sponsors and administration.

Interests of the primary groups who participate in evaluation vary. The evaluator may be concerned with the generalization of his or her findings to other programs and with the production of a piece of work that is respectable to his or her professional colleagues. Program staff is most interested in rendering services to its clientele and may view evaluation as an encroachment on staff time; program sponsors may be most interested in program expenditures and efficiency. With the cooperation of these groups in the planning for evaluation, the results of evaluation are more likely to be understood and used.

The Political Process in Evaluation

In a study that reviewed five planning efforts in community health, Ralph Conant[6] concluded that the

---

[6] Ralph W. Conant, *The Politics of Community Health* (Washington, D.C.: National Commission on Community Health Services, Public Affairs Press, 1968).

major constraints on community-health planning are political. Referring to *political* as the conflict between power groups, he points out that planners must deal with interest-group pressures and counterpressures that arise in negotiations necessary for implementing a plan.

Since evaluations provide information that can be used for planning, it is not surprising that evaluations are also influenced by political considerations. Thus, for example, the Westinghouse evaluation of Head Start programs in 1969 became controversial because it did not produce convincing evidence that Head Start programs were effective, after they had been endorsed by a variety of interest groups as the most popular of the OEO programs.[7]

Some programs are opposed, or heartily endorsed, irrespective of program accomplishments. In addition to Head Start, there are other programs that represent interests of different pressure groups: summer recreation programs intended to keep people off the streets so they will not riot; job-training programs; and so forth. Such programs are often influenced by political decisions and compromises. They may be pet projects of influential groups, political tradeoffs, or token efforts to indicate interest in certain groups. Evaluations of such programs are influenced by the political process and may be encouraged or discouraged as a result of the relative power positions of those for or against the programs.

Just as political realities are necessary considerations in

---

[7] Walter Williams and John W. Evans, "The Politics of Evaluation: The Case of Head Start," *The Annals of the American Academy of Political and Social Science* 385 (September 1969): 118–32.

the planning of social programs, they are also important in evaluation. Program directors must engage in the process of negotiation and change among relevant pressure groups in the operation of their programs. Program directors usually are more skilled than evaluators in working within the political processes that directly involve their programs. Therefore, their skills should be included in the planning of an evaluation. Naive evaluators without political sophistication may draw up evaluation plans that are irrelevant and unrealistic for decision makers. Thus we advocate clarity in negotiations among program staff, evaluators, and other principal interest groups before the conduct of an evaluation.

THE POTENTIAL OF EVALUATION

Differential evaluation can provide useful information about social programs. This result is most probable when the sociopolitical climate is conducive to honest inquiry so there is a commitment to the use of evaluation as a management tool for expanding knowledge and making decisions about social programs. An obvious precondition for evaluation, then, is a state of uncertainty about the social program and the felt need to reduce that uncertainty. Although evaluation studies do not produce *absolutely certain* information about the achievement of program objectives, they can provide relatively objective data that reduce the uncertainty about program achievements. The knowledge derived from evaluation studies ranges in its degree of relative certainty from hypotheses and simple facts to verified hypotheses that can be generalized to a variety of situations. This information can be used for program planning, staff development, and the reporting of program assets and liabilities to various groups to which the program is accountable.

By contrast, evaluation is least likely to provide useful information for developing and modifying social programs in situations such as the following:

1. Evaluation is used as a last resort by administrators to force staff consistency.
2. Evaluation is used solely as a device for compiling information about the incompetence of selected individuals with the general purpose of discrediting those individuals.
3. Evaluation is used as a device selectively to collect *only* information that supports or undermines a social program.

In our view, abuses of evaluation such as those listed above lead to skepticism and cynicism concerning evaluation studies. In the chapters that follow, we provide a framework for program directors so they can plan for useful evaluations. Toward this end, our purpose is to increase the potential of evaluation with the hope that the results of evaluation studies will be used more effectively.

BIBLIOGRAPHY

Ferman, Louis A. "Some Perspectives on Evaluating Social Welfare Programs." *The Annals of the American Academy of Political and Social Science* 385 (September 1969): 143–56.

Guttentag, Marcia, and Struening, Elmer L., eds. *Handbook of Evaluation Research.* Vol. 2. Beverly Hills, Calif.: Sage Publications, 1975.

Hage, Jerald, and Aiken, Michael. *Social Change in Complex Organizations.* New York: Random House, 1970.

Riecken, Henry W., and Boruch, Robert F., eds. *Social Experimentation,* pp. 203–44. New York: Academic Press, 1974.

Struening, Elmer L., and Guttentag, Marcia, eds. *Handbook of Evaluation Research.* Vol. 1. Beverly Hills, Calif.: Sage Publications, 1975.

Tripodi, Tony. "How Handy Is a Handbook." *Contemporary Psychology* 21, no. 10 (1976): 717–19.

Tripodi, Tony; Epstein, Irwin; and MacMurray, Carol. "Dilemmas in Evaluation: Implications for Administrators of Social Action Programs." *American Journal of Orthopsychiatry,* October 1970, pp. 850–57.

Weiss, Carol H. "Evaluation Research in the Political Context." In *Handbook of Evaluation Research.* Vol. 1, pp. 13–26. Edited by Elmer L. Struening and Marcia Guttentag. Beverly Hills, Calif.: Sage Publications, 1975.

Chapter Two

PROGRAM DEVELOPMENT

In the previous chapter, the idea was introduced that social programs move through similar stages of development—program initiation, program contact, and program implementation. Moreover, it was suggested that the current stage of a program, or the stage to which it is attempting to move, will determine which of a wide range of evaluation objectives and evaluation strategies should be applied to it. This matching of evaluation objectives and strategies to a stage of program development is called *differential evaluation*. In this chapter, the notion of program development is described in greater detail as it applies to specific health, education, and welfare programs. Some guidelines are offered for identifying program stages. The relation between program stage and evaluation objectives is taken up in the following chapter.

STAGES OF PROGRAM DEVELOPMENT

Programs can be considered organized efforts to accomplish planned objectives. Those programs concerned with health, education, and welfare vary in many ways. Aside from substantive differences, they vary in the degree to which they are committed to single versus multiple goals. In the field of education, for example, a tutorial program may be designed for the single purpose of increasing reading ability in a given population. By contrast, Project Head Start was designed to achieve multiple purposes—for example, increasing low-income children's psychological readiness for school; increasing low-income parents' participation in and concern about their children's education; and providing health examinations, treatment, and so on. Likewise, health programs may be set up simply to provide chest X-rays or vaccinations, on the one hand, or to provide comprehensive medical care for people, on the other.

Programs also vary in the complexity of their technologies. A food-stamp program, for example, does not rely on the manipulation of a highly complex technology to achieve its goals. Here the problem is often simply one of dissemination of information and of the stamps themselves. Alternatively, a psychiatric clinic makes use of highly complex techniques for selecting, diagnosing, treating, and discharging its clientele.

Other bases of program variation are size, longevity, degree of centralization, type of physical plant and location, and so on. Despite these differences, however, all social programs solve similar developmental problems. First, they must be able to secure sufficient material, social, and technological resources to initiate a program. Second, they must make contact with their designated clientele. Third, they must effectively supply a service or apply a technology, or both, to their individual, group, or organizational clientele.

Before discussing program stages in greater detail, some qualifiers regarding program development are in order. First, neither the complexity of program goals and/or technology nor the length of time a program has been in existence is necessarily an indication of more advanced stages of program development. Thus, for example, a highly complex open-heart surgery program and facility may never transcend the problem of recruitment, training, and maintenance of staff sufficiently skilled to implement the program. Family-service agencies, as another example, may have great longevity and few problems in contacting middle-income clients, but much difficulty in effectively engaging low-income clientele. The causes of such failure in program contact may be many; however, the essential point is that longevity and complexity are not indicative of the stage of program development.

Second, different programs within the same agency may be in different stages of development. A public school may be effectively implementing an educational program for "normal" youngsters at the same time it is attempting to initiate a special-education program for the orthopedically handicapped. Each of these programs requires evaluation in terms of its own stage of development.

Third, it is important to note that not all programs simply progress linearly from one stage to another through time. In fact, the same program can be simultaneously in two or more stages. A public-welfare agency, for example, must simultaneously handle the problems of staff recruitment and training, client contact, and service implementation. Some programs progress in a kind of spiral pattern. A welfare-rights organization may recruit workers to organize welfare recipients to secure more services that will in turn be used as a resource for recruitment of new members, and so on. In each of the above situations, judgments must be made about which stage (or stages) of development is dominant or which stage offers the greatest difficulty.

Fourth, some programs may be concerned entirely and appropriately with their success in making contact with their clientele. This is true when the implementation of program content has already proved to be effective in achieving ultimate program goals. For example, administrators of a program to bring food to starving children in underdeveloped areas may not wish to evaluate the effects of milk and other foodstuffs on the physical health of recipients. More likely they will be interested in measuring the extent to which food reaches its designated clientele instead of going into the local black market.

Despite the foregoing qualifications, almost all social programs are involved in solving sequentially the problems of program initiation, contact, and implementation; and a program must effectively deal with each of these stages before it can move on to the next. The unique problems and characteristics of each stage and their relationship to health, education, and welfare programs are explored in some detail below.

PROGRAM INITIATION

Program initiation is the first stage of program development. It is during this stage that necessary material, social, and technological resources are secured. Although initiation activities vary from program to program, all social programs must deal with the problems of procuring or developing competent staff, financial and physical resources, and social legitimation. Also included in this stage is the planning process: determining a need for the program; specifying program objectives and appropriate technologies for reaching these objectives; identifying a target client population of individuals or organizations and establishing eligibility criteria; spelling out staff functions, personnel policies and practices; and so forth.

These activities represent a necessary part of initiating any social program. Some specific examples of program-initiation problems in health, education, and welfare programs are presented below.

Examples of Program Initiation

Health: A community-based public-health organization decides to try to educate the surrounding community regarding the advantages of fluoridation as a means of reducing tooth decay. The organization may undertake a survey of the attitudes of the general public on this issue. If a need for such a program of education is established, a competent staff will have to be recruited to bring the issue to the community. Decisions about the most effective strategies for involving the community, the techniques for neutralizing the arguments of groups opposed to such a plan, and so on will have to be made. In addition, staff are likely to be involved in locating or developing appropriate source materials to use in bringing their message to the public. Offices, telephones, and meeting places will be required. Moreover, legitimation of the program by local professionals or professional associations may be necessary

Education: An Upward Bound program is proposed for a particular secondary school in a low-income area. The purpose of the program is to identify low-income children who have the intellectual potential for college but lack the necessary economic and social resources. Program initiation in this case involves decisions about the bases for determination of eligibility; the use of existing secondary-school staff, or the hiring of new staff to administer the program; the procurement of material resources for economic support of college-bound youngsters; and so forth. Program strategies will have to be developed to change the attitudes of youngsters who might not ordinarily anticipate going to college. In addition, remedial programming in reading comprehension and written expression is likely to be needed. Thus, before the first potential client is contacted, the program administrator must establish the necessary conditions and make the necessary decisions for initiating the program.

Welfare: A public-welfare agency is required to institute a work-incentive program (WIN) for public-welfare recipients. Since the federal government will be providing the financial resources, the problems of initiation will more likely be related to development of criteria for eligibility for the program, and decisions about the kinds of job-training programs that will have to be developed. In addition, a major effort toward procurement of employment opportunities will have to be made. For all of these decision-making tasks and their implementation, a competent staff will have to be selected. Career lines will have to be developed for these workers as well as for their clients.

PROGRAM CONTACT

Program contact is the second stage of program development. After the objectives of the program-initiation stage are accomplished, contact must be made with potential program beneficiaries. Efforts to contact potential clients may involve mass-media advertisements, door-to-door canvassing, a word-of-mouth campaign, flyers in mailboxes, contacts with personnel in other agencies who may be sources of referrals, and so forth.

Direct contact may take place in different locations. Some agencies employ "outreach" programs that bring the program to the homes in the client community. Other programs make use of intermediary facilities such as "bloodmobiles" that are moveable but require equipment and facilities not readily available in peoples' homes. Still other programs make contact with their potential clients within the office of the sponsoring agency. Despite these differences in technique and location of program contact, all health, education, and welfare agencies must somehow solve the problem of bringing their services or technologies to their clients or client organizations. If these services or technologies cannot be brought to the clientele, the clientele must be brought to the sponsoring agency. Here, program administrators and planners must concern themselves with the physical, material, and social factors that prevent or facilitate program contact.

For the agencies that are more successful in recruiting applicants, the program-contact stage may also involve screening out the applicant individuals, groups, or organizations that are defined as ineligible for program benefits. Public-welfare departments devote much of their staff time and effort to establishing and reestablishing the eligibility of welfare recipients. Teaching hospitals, in screening potential patients, give attention to whether patients' problems make for interesting teaching material. State mental hospitals should, ideally, concern themselves with screening out those potential patients who are not in need of institutionalization or who would be more appropriately served by another facility, for example, an institution for the retarded. On another level, organizations that formally certify professional schools give considerable attention to establishing the eligibility of teaching institutions, since only those schools that meet eligibility criteria receive certification.

The foregoing suggests that, despite their differences, all social programs are involved in the successful attainment of program contact. Administrators approach this with an eye to the program's ultimate goals and the availability of program resources. Some detailed examples of program contact follow.

Examples of Program Contact

Health: A TB control unit of a state department of health has as one of its purposes the reduction of tuberculosis in poor urban communities. Accomplishment of program contact requires the designated target population to receive chest X-rays. Past experience suggests, however, that a clinic program in a downtown public hospital is not successful in attracting the target population, since some of these people cannot take the time or do not have the carfare to travel to the clinic, and others do not read about the program in the newspaper and consequently have no knowledge of it. Still others, perhaps suspecting that they have TB and fearful of the stigma or the treatment, are reluctant to be identified by public-health officials. So, as an alternative program-contact strategy, program planners decide to institute a mobile X-ray unit to bring doctors, technicians, and X-ray facilities directly to the client community. Other social agencies are informed of this new service and the dates when the mobile unit will be in the area. The time, effort, and the social costs of the examinations are reduced and the visibility of the program is increased.

Education: An adult-education program has as one of its purposes the improvement of the English-language skills of recent, non-English-speaking immigrants. Program contact will necessitate decisions about how to inform the recent immigrants that the program is available, for example, through advertisements in foreign-language newspapers or contacts with appropriate nationality organizations. In addition, attention must be given to the physical location of the program and the times when classes are to be held. The merits of segregating nationality or language groups, versus mixing them in classes, will also have to be considered. Should the program be free to all participants, or should all participants pay a standard fee, or should the fee be determined on the basis of income? These decisions, and others as well, are likely to affect the success with which the program manages to contact its clientele.

Welfare: A settlement house decides to organize a welfare council in a given community. The goal is to coordinate the planning of the various social-welfare agencies in the area. Program contact involves decisions about how to contact the potential member agencies. How do the program's administrators communicate their objectives to decision makers in the various organizations so the program will present no threat and will offer some incentive for membership? Are meetings to be held in the sponsoring agency, or will they take place elsewhere in the community? Are meetings to be held at times when representatives of all significant agencies can attend?

How the program planners answer these questions will significantly determine how well the program-contact stage is managed.

PROGRAM IMPLEMENTATION

Program implementation is the third stage of program development. In this final stage, the program fully engages its clientele and gives service and/or applies a change technology. The success of program implementation rests in part on the attainment of the necessary conditions of program initiation and contact. It also depends on the relevancy of the service offered or on the efficacy of the technology employed. Thus, program implementation overlaps with and is a result of effective program contacts.

The purpose of the program-implementation stage is synonymous with the ultimate goals of the program. It is here that the *outcome* of program planning can be measured. Questions about unanticipated positive and negative consequences of program interventions can also be answered during program implementation. In addition, this stage offers a locus in which the relative efficacy and efficiency of the program's various strategies can be evaluated.

In some programs, a necessary part of the implementation stage is the disengagement of clientele. Criteria for their discharge and a technology for handling them must be developed. A state mental hospital can be said to be truly successful only when it has successfully reintegrated its patients into the society. A job-training program for low-income people must be able to place trainees in meaningful positions where the skills they learned are, in fact, used. A correctional institution, to the extent that it focuses on rehabilitation, must concern itself with the reintegration of ex-convicts into the larger noncriminal community.

But disengagement can also be premature. It is possible, for example, that some organizations release their clientele before they are properly serviced or treated. Along these lines, some public-welfare agencies have been accused of giving more attention to cutting clients off the welfare rolls than to servicing them. This issue suggests important questions for evaluation. More detailed examples follow.

Examples of Program Implementation

Health: A prenatal-care clinic is set up for pregnant women in a low-income community. The goal of the program is to reduce the incidence of stillborn, premature, and defective infants in the area. The program director has acquired the resources successfully to initiate the program and to make contact with clientele. He is, however, concerned with the degree to which clients regularly keep their appointments, follow dietary instructions and other medical advice. Ultimately, of course, he is concerned with the extent to which there have been decreases in the birth rates of stillborn, premature, and defective infants in the area. Some secondary gains, which might result from the program, could involve improved health-care practices of the clients, such as the reduction of smoking or better dietary habits. In addition, the original clients might refer other women to the program, contributing to the program's success in contacting a larger potential clientele. Certain unanticipated negative consequences might result from an increased number of illegitimate children who might otherwise have died in childbirth: added pressures on families, schools, and other local institutions.

Education: A public-school system initiates a guidance and counseling program within its schools. Ample staff and material resources are available. Teachers have been cooperative and judicious in referring children with personal and social problems to the school guidance personnel. Ultimately, the question facing the program administrator is whether intervention has been successful in reducing school-related behavior problems. In addition, it would be helpful to find out whether behavior problems outside the context of the school were also reduced. In considering unanticipated negative consequences, it would be important to note whether teachers' classroom behavior has changed negatively as a result of the availability of the program. Have they become less tolerant of minor infractions of rules? Have they been less willing to work with children manifesting behavior difficulties? The program administrator might also investigate the differential effects of having the social workers function as consultants to teachers or as direct counselors to troubled youngsters.

Welfare: A food-stamp program is set up in a community, with the purpose of enabling local residents to have nutritionally adequate diets. The stamps, providing for foodstuffs that are compatible with the tastes and customs of the people in the area, are distributed regularly, and neighborhood food stores agree to accept the stamps. In this stage, the program director is interested in how people actually use the stamps and whether the nutritional value of their diets does improve. In addition, it would be valuable to know whether participation in the program leads to greater interest in good nutrition and better planning in the selection of foods. On the negative side, one would want to know whether local stores raise their prices when stamps are distributed and whether they allow customers to purchase nonprescribed products with their stamps, such as sweets, soft drinks, and alcohol.

DETERMINATION OF PROGRAM STAGES[1]

Although it is obvious that there are often no clear lines of demarcation between program stages, our purpose in delineating developmental stages is to make evaluation more relevant to the current state of a program. Differential evaluation then requires that the present developmental stage (or stages) of the program be identified. But how can the program administrator make this determination? Listed below are some guidelines for

---

[1] Many of the ideas in this section were derived from Amitai Etzioni, *Modern Organizations* (Englewood Cliffs, N.J.: Prentice-Hall, 1964).

identifying the developmental stage(s) that dominates a social program.[2]

1. How does the program allocate most of its staff time and resources? Are present efforts devoted to securing additional resources (initiation), recruiting clientele (contact), or giving service and/or applying a technology (implementation)?
2. When there are conflicts between the needs of the various program stages, how are these resolved? Which stage generally dominates?
3. What kinds of data and information does the program routinely collect? Does the intelligence system focus mainly on data concerning the availability of new program resources (initiation), description of clientele (contact), or impact on clientele of agency intervention (implementation)?
4. What kinds of staff activity receive the greatest economic and status rewards? What roles are viewed as most valuable to the program operation?
5. If there were a major cutback in funding, which functions would be sacrificed first; which last?

Each of the foregoing questions directs the administrator to a determination of the current "operative goals" of the program, and to the dominant stage(s) of program development. These operative goals may coincide or

---

[2] A dominant program stage is that stage to which more than 50 per cent of program activities, efforts, and resources are devoted. Two or more stages may be sufficiently overlapping within a particular program so there may be no single dominant stage. In that instance, the administrator would regard both stages as representative of the state of program development.

depart from "stated" program goals, that is, goals presented in formal program documents, mandates, contracts, and so forth. They do, however, tell the administrator where the program is at any time.

BIBLIOGRAPHY

Beckhard, Richard. *Organization Development: Strategies and Models.* Reading, Mass.: Addison-Wesley, 1970.

Bennett, Eleanor C., and Weisinger, Marvin. *Program Evaluation: A Resource Handbook for Vocational Rehabilitation,* pp. 9–19. New York: ICD Rehabilitation and Research Center, 1974.

Donabedian, Avedis. *A Guide to Medical Care Administration.* Vol. II of *Medical Care Appraisal.* Washington, D.C.: American Public Health Association, 1969.

Etzioni, Amitai. *Modern Organizations.* Englewood Cliffs, N.J.: Prentice-Hall, 1964.

Hage, Jerald, and Aiken, Michael. *Social Change in Complex Organizations,* pp. 9–25. New York: Random House, 1970.

Chapter Three

EVALUATION OBJECTIVES
AND QUESTIONS

In chapter 2, we described three stages of program development: program initiation, program contact, and program implementation. The purpose of this chapter is to provide the program director with a framework for formulating evaluation objectives appropriate to the program's developmental stage. This framework is based on our notion of *differential evaluation,* which means simply that an evaluation of a social program should be geared primarily to the present stage (or stages) of program development. In this context, different evaluation questions are suggested for different program stages; the range of evaluation strategies for answering these questions is considered in subsequent chapters.

EVALUATION OBJECTIVES

Differential evaluation involves the location and selection of evaluation strategies for answering evaluation questions for stages of program development. Within each program stage three objectives or criteria of evaluation should be considered: program effort, program effectiveness, and program efficiency. Essentially, then, there are three basic objectives of program evaluation:

1. To provide descriptive information about the type and quantity of program activities or inputs (*program effort*)
2. To provide information about the achievement of the goals of the current stage of program development (*program effectiveness*)
3. To provide information about program effectiveness relative to program effort (*program efficiency*)

A program evaluation that does not include systematic information about effort, effectiveness, and efficiency is incomplete.[1] For example, knowledge about program efforts without corresponding knowledge about the achievement of the goals of a particular stage of development is relatively useless to the administrator who must make decisions about continuing or altering

---

[1] Incomplete evaluations, for example, those that focus on effectiveness only, may be useful if the administrator already has knowledge regarding the other criteria of evaluation, or if there are plans to secure such knowledge in separate evaluation studies.

present strategies of intervention. He or she needs answers to questions about which activities should be increased or curtailed; which activities bring about desired ends; whether there should be a shift in program emphasis; and so on. Likewise, information about the achievement of program objectives must be related to program effort. In this way the administrator can make judgments about the relative costs and efficiency of various intervention strategies. Thus, the issues of effort, effectiveness, and efficiency are different but necessarily interrelated. Each of these criteria of evaluation are discussed here.

Program Effort

Evaluation of *program effort* refers to an assessment of the amounts and kinds of program activities considered necessary for the accomplishment of program goals within a particular stage of development. It refers not only to staff time, activity, and commitment, but also to the allocation and use of material resources—funds, space, equipment, and so on. For example, in a marital counseling program in the program-contact stage, information such as the following might be obtained about program effort: what techniques for recruiting potential clientele have been employed; how much staff time, effort, funds, and so on have been expended; and what ancillary resources have been used—for example, outside consultation, media, public relations, and so on?

Program effort can be documented in any developmental stage. Essentially, this quantitative, descriptive information is an indication of the extent to which staff and program are active. Obviously, this says nothing about how well the tasks are being done or, more importantly, whether the program's overall goals are being attained. However, if there is little effort invested in a program, little can be accomplished; directors may be very interested in finding out whether staff are actively engaged in the program. Thus, program effort is necessary for the achievement of program goals, but evidence of program activity is not sufficient to determine whether these goals have been reached.

Information about program effort may be extremely useful to administrators in situations in which the relationship between intervention techniques and desired outcomes has been fairly firmly established. For example, a reading tutorial program has been set up to employ techniques of reading instruction that have been successfully initiated, and program contact has been made. An analysis of staff activity, however, reveals that staff is devoting a major proportion of its time and effort to recreational activities for individuals in the program. With this information, and after some thought to the reasons for the inappropriate character of staff activities (e.g., inadequate training in implementing the techniques of reading instruction), the administrator attempts to increase the proportion of staff time devoted to instructional activities. His or her decision is based on the assumption that these techniques of reading instruction will in fact lead to improved reading levels.

Of course, the program administrator may also be

interested in evaluating the effectiveness of these techniques *within* his program. He may have reason to believe, for example, that the clientele served may be sufficiently different from that served in other programs (e.g., cultural or ethnic differences) so the effectiveness of the means employed should not be taken as assumed. If he has information indicative of program effectiveness, he can be more certain of the correctness of his decisions about the allocation of agency resources.

Program Effectiveness

As with program effort, program effectiveness can be determined for any given stage of development. *Effectiveness* refers to the extent to which the goals of a particular stage have been achieved. For example, a community-based agency hopes to organize local re- sources to get a Model Cities Program operating in the area. To implement such a program, certain initiation activities must be successfully managed. A planning grant must be secured; a group of experts and local citizens must be brought together to document the need for such a project and plan a program; a representative board must be recruited and established; and so forth. Effectiveness in the initiation stage would refer to the success with which each of these foregoing requirements has been managed.

In addition to the above, an evaluation of effectiveness would consider both desirable and undesirable unantici- pated consequences (i.e., results of programs that were not planned by program staff) that may result from program activities. In the case of the initiation of a Model Cities Program, for example, an evaluator would be interested in the extent to which efforts for securing necessary resources to initiate such a program promoted either community cohesiveness or conflict. Are local residents becoming more active in community affairs unrelated to model cities? Are local community organizations and agencies fighting over available resources or coordinating and integrating their programs and services?

Program effectiveness may also include information that bears on the achievement of program goals in relation to the need for the program. For example, each of two similar health programs in two communities may have provided services to 100 families. One community (A) may have had 1,000 families in need of health services, and the other community (B) may have had 100 families that could benefit from health services. Thus, the services in community B are more comprehensive in that the ratio between those served and those in need (100/100) is higher than it is for community A (100/1,000). Comprehensiveness is an index of effectiveness, which relates goal achievement to community needs; it indicates the *impact* a program has on the community in which it is located.

Information regarding effectiveness is typically quantitative, but qualitative data that reflect on effectiveness may also be secured in program evaluations. For example, included in the objectives of some programs may be such items as the procurement of "adequate" physical facilities; compliance with regulations and local ordinances regarding discrimination, equal opportunity practices, personnel policies, and housing codes; the procurement of "adequate" ratios of staff to people served, such as those for teachers and students, physicians and patients. Such information is often judged by the standards of professionals, who may base their judgments on previous experience, knowledge, and current professional norms. Those kinds of data are more often used in evaluating objectives in the program initiation and contact stages of development; and they, along with information regarding the availability and accessibility of services, as well as the responsiveness and humaneness of program staff in its dealings with clientele, can be regarded as indices of *quality*. However, qualitative information is also used in evaluating the effectiveness of program implementation.

Two alternative program approaches may lead to the same degree of effectiveness, but the expenditure of resources in one program may be greater than in the other. An important item of information for the administrator, then, is the relative cost for accomplishing program objectives. Other things being equal, the administrator would choose the program that is the least costly in terms of time, money, manpower, and other resources. Thus, program efficiency is another important object of evaluation.

Program Efficiency

Program efficiency focuses on the relationship between efforts and effectiveness. Two indicators of this relationship are the ratio of effectiveness to efforts, and the difference between effectiveness and efforts. Efficiency is an index of the relative costs for achieving program objectives, where costs include expenditures of manpower, time, money, physical facilities, and so forth.

Questions regarding efficiency are familiar to administrators who are involved in making programmatic decisions within the constraints of relatively fixed budgets. Evaluation of efficiency often involves comparison of two or more techniques (or strategies, or programs) with respect to their relative costs and program outcomes. However, questions may also be raised about duplications of effort, irrespective of whether one has knowledge of the effectiveness of those efforts. To illustrate the point, a program may employ ten persons to determine whether applicants are eligible for its services. If all ten persons interview the *same* applicants, there is an unnecessary duplication of efforts. The less duplication of effort, the more efficient the program. The notion of duplication of efforts can be expanded to include office procedures, the use of meetings and committees, and so forth.

As indicated previously, questions of efficiency need not be focused directly on financial costs. For example, the use of time is important information for the administrator, for time expended can be converted to costs by multiplying staff salaries by the proportions of time devoted to various program activities. How much time is spent in the teaching of groups as opposed to tutorials? Can an interview devoted to determining eligibility of program applicants be concluded in one hour as opposed to three hours?

The essence of an evaluation of efficiency is highlighted in this question: can the same program results be achieved *either* by reducing the amount of program effort *or* by choosing other, less costly alternatives (different kinds of efforts)? It must be emphasized that a reduction of program costs that leads to a corresponding reduction in effectiveness does not make a program more efficient. Program A may be twice as costly as Program B, and it may also be twice as effective; hence, the two programs are equally efficient.

EVALUATION QUESTIONS AND PROGRAM DEVELOPMENT

The objective of differential evaluation is to produce sets of data on the efforts, effectiveness, and efficiency of achieving program goals. Evaluation questions geared to different stages of development represent specifications of this objective. To illustrate more systematically the linkage between the stages of development and the evaluation questions, the following section offers some evaluation questions that can be asked of social programs in the different developmental stages. The questions are intended to serve as illustrative guidelines. Before the delineation of more general evaluation questions, we also offer brief examples of evaluation questions applied to specific social programs.

Program Initiation

As we discussed in chapter 2, the goals in the program-initiation stage are concentrated on securing the necessary resources and conditions for client contact and program implementation. An example of a social program in the initiation stage might be a job-training program proposed for public-welfare recipients in a particular community, with the ultimate goal of helping recipients to be financially independent. Immediate goals in the initiation stage are focused on the selection and recruitment of competent staff, the determination of necessary criteria for eligibility, and so on. To formulate evaluation objectives it is necessary to specify questions related to the effort, effectiveness, and efficiency with which the tasks of the initiation stage are managed. Questions such as the following might be raised to evaluate program efforts: what attempts were made to secure staff persons to operate the program; and how much time, energy, and other resources were devoted to the specification of eligibility criteria, such as the educational level necessary to benefit from the program?

Questions regarding program effectiveness are related to the extent to which program efforts result in the achievement of program goals. Thus, the following questions of effectiveness can be raised: were sufficient numbers of staff persons hired in accordance with their planned qualifications; were criteria developed for the unbiased selection of program participants; and were adequate accounting, bookkeeping, and social data-recording procedures established?

Program efficiency of the job-training program might be evaluated with respect to questions such as these: if different methods for the recruitment of staff are used, which method is most efficient in terms of length of time for recruitment and the costs of program efforts; and to what extent is the content of training relevant to the job market (e.g., training for secretarial work when no jobs in the community are available for secretaries)?

Illustrative Evaluation Questions: Program Initiation

EFFORT

1. How much time and activity are devoted to the recruitment of staff for the program?
2. What is the extent and the type of activity devoted to the location of resources and the procurement of program cooperation?
3. What is the extent of involvement in the development of personnel policies and practices and adequate accounting, bookkeeping, and data-collection procedures?
4. What are the number and nature of activities devoted to the development of an operational plan, the review of existing programs of a similar nature, a review of the literature for alternative approaches, and interviews with persons who have experience in similar programs?
5. To what extent are efforts made to define and locate the potential target population?
6. What efforts are focused on the learning of statutes, ordinances, and regulations relevant to the program?

EFFECTIVENESS

1. Are there any staff vacancies; how many of the filled positions are a result of recruiting efforts?
2. To what extent do community residents perceive the program as related to community needs? To what extent can potential participants be identified; would those persons be willing to participate in the program?
3. To what extent is a program plan specified, including its objectives and alternative ways to accomplish those objectives?
4. To what extent are budgeting, accounting, and data-collection procedures established in accordance with acceptable practices?
5. To what extent are personnel policies and practices explicated and consistent with relevant laws and guidelines?
6. To what extent are staff functions and responsibilities delineated?

EFFICIENCY

1. What are the relative costs of different procedures for the recruitment of staff?
2. In comparison to existing programs of a similar nature, what are the relative costs for the initiation stage of the program?
3. To what extent are staff salaries commensurate with

the responsibilities of staff positions, in relation to similar jobs in the community?

4. To what extent are there duplicated staff functions that could result in possible ambiguity and conflict?

5. To what extent do staff persons perceive program objectives as similar or dissimilar; to what extent do staff persons have competing objectives that are at cross purposes with one another?

6. To what extent are program activities related to program objectives and/or to program survival?

Program Contact

The goals of the contact stage are concerned with the bringing together of program content and clientele. Immediate objectives are focused on the identification of favorable and unfavorable conditions for program contacts. Accordingly, evaluation questions are geared to the efforts, effectiveness, and efficiency with which program contact is managed. For example, a social program in the contact stage might be one in which a public-health program is initiated for the purpose of locating and treating venereal disease in the teenage population. Evaluation questions related to effort are as follows: how much manpower time is expended to reach the target population; what techniques and media are used to make initial contact; and so forth.

Effectiveness might be assessed by providing answers to questions such as these: what proportion of the target population knows about the program; and how willing are they to come in for initial examinations?

Questions of efficiency are those that involve the relation of staff efforts to the achievement of the goal of client contact. Are there less costly, but equally or more effective, uses of media and modes of dissemination of information, uses of staff, and so on for contacting clientele?

Illustrative Evaluation Questions: Program Contact

EFFORT

1. What amounts of time and program resources are devoted to making program contacts with intended beneficiaries: number of interviews, and so on?
2. If a referral system is used, what is the amount of time and effort involved in referrals?
3. What efforts are devoted to the compilation of records pertaining to program activity?
4 What amounts of time and activity are devoted to finding resources that could increase the number of program contacts?
5. To what extent are alternative program strategies sought and used, if program efforts do not appear sufficient to reach all of the intended target population?

EFFECTIVENESS

1. To what extent is the intended target population

represented in those who are designated as program beneficiaries?

2. What are the opinions of the intended target population regarding the extent to which the content of the program is reaching them and the reasons why program contacts are or are not made?

3. What is the number of appropriate services used, out of the possible number of available referral sources; what are the reasons for the use (or lack of use) of referral services?

4. What happens to prospective clientele who are referred to other programs; how many persons actually receive services from the programs to which they are referred?

5. What is the extent of unsuccessful completions of service or premature terminations, that is, dropouts?

EFFICIENCY

1. What are the relative proportions of staff time devoted to program objectives, and to what extent is the use of staff time related to the achievement of those objectives?

2. What are the relative costs of using different means for contacting clientele?

3. Are staff functions and roles structured to maximize program consistency for the achievement of program goals?

4. Are certain client characteristics more related to program contact than others; for example, do

whites receive more or less program contact than blacks?

5. Are certain staff characteristics more related to program contacts than others?

6. Are certain staff or client characteristics related to program dropouts?

Program Implementation

Program implementation involves the achievement of, or failure to achieve, ultimate program goals. For an education program that attempts to increase the education level of adults from below third-grade to an eighth-grade level, evaluation questions of effort might include the following: how many hours of instruction were provided for what specific skills, such as reading and arithmetic; what devices were considered, and actually used, for assessing the educational level of program beneficiaries; and so forth.

Questions of effectiveness might include the following: how many program beneficiaries actually increased their educational levels in reading, arithmetic, and so on; what proportion of the intended target population increased their educational levels; and how many persons dropped out of the program and for what reasons?

Efficiency might be appraised by seeking information through questions such as these: is group teaching less costly and equally as effective as tutorials; and could the same degree of effectiveness be obtained by less costly means through the use of nonprofessional teachers, teaching machines, and so on.

Illustrative Evaluation Questions: Program Implementation

EFFORT

1. How much time and energy are devoted to a review of staff objectives and activities?
2. What staff efforts are involved in the respecification of goals, and in the location of additional resources judged necessary to achieve program results?
3. How much effort is devoted to the specification of criteria for program termination and necessary follow-up activities?
4. How much time and activity are devoted to the procurement of follow-up information from program beneficiaries?
5. How much effort is devoted to the consideration and specification of policies for the reentry of dropouts?

EFFECTIVENESS

1. What results have been achieved that could be attributed to the program; are there discernible changes in the knowledge, attitudes, or skills of the program beneficiaries; are there changes in behavior on the part of individuals, groups, or organizations?
2. What results could have been obtained without the content of the program (would changes have taken place anyway)?

3. Are there any unplanned outcomes, either desirable or undesirable, that could be attributed to the program?
4. How effective is the program in relation to the need of the intended target population?

EFFICIENCY

1. What are the relative costs of different techniques used to achieve similar results?
2. What is the relation of costs of program effort to the benefits of results achieved?
3. What are the relative costs of the program in comparison with other programs with similar objectives?
4. Could the same results be achieved with a reduction in program efforts?

BIBLIOGRAPHY

Glaser, Daniel. *Routinizing Evaluation: Getting Feedback on Effectiveness of Crime and Delinquency Programs.* DHEW Publication No. (HSM) 73-9123, pp. 16–25. Rockville, Md.: National Institute of Mental Health, 1973.

Levin, Henry M. "Cost-Effectiveness Analyses in Evaluation Research." In *Handbook of Evaluation Research.* Vol. 2, pp. 89–124. Edited by Marcia Guttentag and Elmer L. Struening.

Beverly Hills, Calif.: Sage Publications, 1975.

Suchman, Edward A. *Evaluative Research,* pp. 51–73. New York: Russell Sage Foundation, 1967.

Twain, David. "Developing and Implementing a Research Strategy." In *Handbook of Evaluation Research.* Vol. 1, pp. 27–52. Edited by Elmer L. Struening and Marcia Guttentag. Beverly Hills, Calif.: Sage Publications, 1975.

Weiss, Carol H. *Evaluation Research,* pp. 24–59. Englewood Cliffs, N. J.: Prentice-Hall. 1972.

Chapter Four

EVALUATION STRATEGIES

After the evaluation objectives have been specified, the next concern in differential evaluation is the selection of appropriate strategies that can be used to provide relatively unbiased information pertinent to the questions of evaluation. Although the typical administrator is not an expert in the technical aspects of evaluation, he is often in a position where he must seek consultation regarding the kind of evaluation strategy that is most appropriate for his program. The task of the administrator is to locate an evaluation expert who is able to select and/or use those techniques, or combinations of techniques, that would yield the desired information at reasonable cost. To locate and use evaluation experts appropriately, however, the administrator should have some acquaintance with the aims of various evaluation strategies.

Accordingly, our goal in this chapter is to acquaint the administrator with the aims of various evaluation strategies; it is *not* to discuss exhaustively the detailed techniques and methods for conducting program evaluations. These strategies can be used at different stages of evaluation for providing information regarding efforts, effectiveness, and efficiency of program goals. These strategies are grouped into three categories: monitoring, social-research, and cost-analytic strategies. *Monitoring strategies* include those procedures used for the direct review of program operations: social accounting, administrative audit, and time-and-motion studies. *Social-research strategies* refer to those procedures, exclusive of cost considerations, used for developing, modifying, and expanding knowledge about the program that can be communicated and verified by independent investigators: experiment, survey, and case study. *Cost-analytic strategies* are those procedures used to appraise the relative value of a program in relation to program costs: general accounting, cost accounting, cost-benefit analyses, and cost-effectiveness analyses.

These categories are overlapping, but they are useful because particular kinds of evaluation experts are often identified with these groupings. Thus, management consultants, accountants, efficiency experts, organizational sociologists, and statisticians may be associated with monitoring techniques; psychologists, sociologists, biostatisticians, and epidemiologists with social-research techniques; and accountants, economists, mathematicians, and systems analysts with cost-analytic techniques.

The purpose of this chapter is to present an overview of

selected evaluation strategies and to include in our brief discussions of each strategy the following: a *description* of the strategy, including its purpose, what experts in the strategy are likely to do, the kinds of knowledge that can be produced by the strategy, and an indication of the relative costs in terms of time, money, and manpower; a discussion of some suggested *uses* of the strategy; and an annotated *bibliography* of selected references from which the reader can derive detailed discussions regarding the implementation of the strategy (i.e., how to do evaluations). Thus, the primary aim is to provide an introduction to various strategies so administrators can be more sensitive to the selection of evaluation consultants. In the next chapter we present guidelines for matching different evaluation strategies to evaluation questions of efforts, effectiveness, and efficiency for each of the program-development stages.

MONITORING STRATEGIES

Social Accounting

DESCRIPTION

Social accounting, often thought of as bookkeeping, "head counting," client-information processing, or agency-descriptive statistics, refers to the methods used by the program for recording and keeping track of program beneficiaries. This accounting system is the source of program statistics on things such as how many persons were contacted by program staff and where contacts were made. The accounting might be done by a systems analyst, statistician, epidemiologist, or social researcher who is expert in the formulation and use of program records for processing client information. The accounting function involves an appraisal of the existence, reliability, and accuracy of the program's procedures for reporting on those persons who have been processed through the program—from recruiting and program-contact efforts to final follow-up. The social accountant looks at the available records in use, such as monthly or daily activity reports; files kept for such records; and any reported statistics regarding program progress. Then he or she checks the records that form the basis for the reported statistics to verify their accuracy. In addition, he or she may review policies, procedures, and definitions of statistical categories. The social accountant attempts to determine whether definitions are ambiguous and whether there appears to be an accurate count of people processed through the program. When numbers are used, but based on varying estimates without documentation, he or she makes a judgment regarding the validity of such numbers (e.g., when a recreation program reports it has processed 10,000 people at a public park during a given month, is that figure based on information that indicates 10,000 different people, or is it the number of days in a month multiplied by how many people a recreation worker believed were at the park on a given day?).

The knowledge obtained from social accounting

includes recommendations for an adequate data-process-ing system. These record-keeping systems contain basic kinds of information essential for program planning, development, and review. The more thorough the system, from intake through follow-up, the more costly it will be. The costs of a social-accounting expert are not exorbitant, but a comprehensive data-recording system is not inexpensive. Much information can be manufac-tured and processed through a computerized data-collection system, but if information is collected without being used, the cost is excessive and unnecessary. Therefore, the role of the social accountant is to recommend which kinds of information pertinent to program goals and evaluation objectives should be collected.

USES

Social-accounting strategies can be used to provide information that bears on efforts, effectiveness, and efficiency of program goals during the three stages of program development. For example, a review of a social program in the initiation stage may indicate whether program efforts have been devoted to the establishment of social-accounting procedures, how effective the program has been in employing an adequate accounting system, and how efficient the system is in terms of duplication of efforts and so forth.

A program in the contact stage cannot have adequate knowledge of its efforts and effectiveness unless the documentation exists in its social-accounting records. Thus, social-accounting strategies can be used to determine whether the program has the necessary procedures for the efficient tabulation of those clients who are processed by the program.

For programs in the implementation stage, administrators often have difficulty in securing follow-up information pertinent to those who have graduated from their program. Social-accounting strategies can be used for recommending ways to process follow-up information. Moreover, they can be used to review the program's efforts to procure such information for data processing.

BIBLIOGRAPHY[1]

Bauer, Raymond A., ed. *Social Indicators* Cambridge, Mass.: The M.I.T. Press, 1966.
    A selection of five articles that deal with the use and planning of social statistical data. Especially recommended for the reader are the sections on "Social Indicators and Goals," by Albert D. Biderman, pp. 68-153, and "The State of the Nation: Social Systems Accounting," by Bertram M. Gross, pp. 154–271.
Epstein, Irwin, and Tripodi, Tony. *Research Techniques for Program Planning, Monitoring*

---

[1] The references included in this and subsequent sections are not intended to be exhaustive. They are principal sources for the authors, and they are merely intended to be suggestive to the reader who wants to delve more deeply into each strategy.

and Evaluation. New York: Columbia University Press, 1977.

Chapters 6 and 7 specify how to develop forms for conducting a client census and for monitoring staff activities.

Livingstone, John L., and Gunn, Sanford C. *Accounting for Social Goals.* New York: Harper and Row, 1974.

Readings on multiple-goal information systems are presented and social issues involved in social accounting are discussed.

Sherwood, Clarence C. "Guidelines for a Data Collection System for Community Programs for Unemployed Youth." Paper prepared for New York University Graduate School of Social Work, Center for the Study of Unemployed Youth, February 1966, 16 pp.

Specific recommendations are made for a data-collection system relevant to the social accountability of social programs.

Weinstein, Abbott S. "Evaluation Through Medical Records and Related Information Systems." In *Handbook of Evaluation Research,* edited by Elmer L. Struening and Marcia Guttentag, pp. 397–481. Beverly Hills, Calif.: Sage Publications, 1975.

A comprehensive discussion of the multistate information system on psychiatric patients and other information systems useful for social accounting is presented.

Administrative Audit

DESCRIPTION

Administrative-audit strategies attempt to describe what is done by staff in relation to standards established by sources external and/or internal to the program. Standards are designated norms of desirable activity, and they may be derived from the professions or other groups; or relative standards may be derived from a systematic comparison with other similar programs or organizations. More specifically, administrative-audit strategies, herein, refer to those procedures used to evaluate the suitability of program policies and practices directed toward compliance with those policies; to evaluate the adherence of staff practices to designated divisions of responsibility and function; and to evaluate the organizational patterns of work in terms of preferred and efficient procedures within the program and/or between the program and other programs of a similar nature.

An administrative auditor might be a management consultant, an expert on administrative procedures, an expert on intraorganizational procedures and systems engineering, or a sociologist who is expert in comparing complex organizations. A comprehensive and detailed administrative audit might require a team of those experts or one or more persons who have a combination of skills such as the ability to analyze management procedures within and between organizations.

An administrative audit might contain any of the following ingredients. The auditor looks for written policies regarding personnel practices, functions, and responsibilities. He or she may determine whether organizational charts are used and to what extent existing staff practices may correspond with those charts. In addition, the auditor looks for internal consistencies and inconsistencies as reflected in the chart and observes whether such ambiguities are reflected in the interviews he or she conducts with staff and in the observations he or she makes. Moreover, the auditor attempts to determine the degree of consistency among those staff members he or she interviews regarding their perceptions of staff functions and responsibilities. Available documents (written policies, codes, minutes of staff meetings, board meeting minutes, etc.) are reviewed with respect to internal consistency and their correspondence with available policies, ordinances, and so on, outside of the program.

The knowledge obtained from an administrative audit is usually in the form of facts pertaining to administrative and staff work patterns and the extent to which the program could improve its goals in relation to its management activities. The management audit can be more limited in perspective and concentrate on developing knowledge that pertains to things such as civil rights compliance, adherence to nondiscriminatory personnel practices, and recommendations for more efficient staff efforts. With a limited audit, the costs are minimal, namely, those of manpower necessary for the audit over a brief period. On the other hand, considerable costs are entailed in comprehensive audits that include the use of a variety of specific techniques (such as PERT, as described in the reference below, to assist in planning the accomplishment of specific tasks in given amounts of time) for appraising the program administration over extended periods and for comparing it with other similar programs.

USES

The information secured by an administrative audit is particularly useful for the planning involved in social programs. Although an administrative audit may be helpful in all stages of program development, it is more useful in the program-initiation and contact stages. As previously indicated, the information gathered by the auditor may be used to form judgments, based on available documentation, regarding discriminatory practice toward employees, lack of compliance with specified regulations, personnel conflicts in the operation of the program, lack of compliance with accepted professional practices, and so forth. Recommendations can then be made concerning the efforts the program should make to be more effective and efficient in its administrative practices. For example, a management audit of the initiation stage of an antipoverty program may reveal the extent to which the program made efforts to secure adequate representation on its policy and planning board (door-to-door house canvassing, advertisements in the media for local elections, etc.); the extent to which recruiting efforts were effective in being nondiscriminatory; and the program's efficiency (unnecessary duplication) in its hiring procedures.

A more comprehensive administrative audit may include recommendations for estimating the number of personnel necessary for providing effective services, as determined by professional judgments of adequate service (e.g., see reference below by Schonfeld et al.), or a comparative analysis of the program's administrative efforts, effectiveness, and efficiency with other programs (e.g., see references below by Perrow, Fanshel, and Terry).

BIBLIOGRAPHY

Epstein, Irwin, and Tripodi, Tony. *Research Techniques for Program Planning, Monitoring and Evaluation*. New York: Columbia University Press, 1977.

A conception of program monitoring is discussed, and selected research techniques that can be applied in administrative audits are included.

Etzioni, Amitai. *Modern Organizations*. Englewood Cliffs, N. J.: Prentice-Hall, 1964.

An excellent and succinct text that presents and reviews concepts for the analysis of complex organizations. In particular, chapter 2, which includes a discussion of the nature of organizational goals and their evaluation, is important background information regarding the nature of different organizations.

Fanshel, David, ed. *Research in Social Welfare Administration: Its Contributions and Problems*. New York: National Association of Social Workers, 1962.

This text includes discussions of major issues regarding research of administration in social work and several suggested techniques for the analysis of different administrative structures. Recommended for the reader are these articles: "The Study of Organizational Effectiveness," by Herman D. Stein, pp. 22–32, and "Research in Administrative Medicine: Comparative Analysis of Systems of Health Service Organizations," by Milton I. Roemer, pp. 72–83.

Perrow, Charles. "A Framework for the Comparative Analysis of Organizations." *American Sociological Review* 32, no. 2 (April 1967): 194–208.

A suggested framework for comparing different social organizations is proposed and discussed.

Pfeiffer, John. *New Look at Education: Systems Analysis in Our Schools and Colleges*. Poughkeepsie, N. Y.: Odyssey Press, 1968.

An interesting and informative discussion of techniques used for analyzing educational institutions is presented. In particular, clear discussions of PERT and other critical path methods for determining efficient and effective time schedules for the completion of projects are provided in chapter 3, pp. 33–53.

Schonfeld, H. K.; Falk, I. S.; Lavietes, P. H.; Landwirth, I.; and Krassnor, L. S. "The Development of Standards for the Audit and Planning of Medical Care." *American Journal of Public Health* 88, no. 11 (November 1968): 2097–110.

The authors describe a technique for deriving and applying standards of good pediatric care for estimating the number of personnel needed to provide adequate care.

Terry, George R. *Principles of Management.* 6th ed. Homewood, Ill.: Richard D. Irwin, 1972.

Recommended are chapters 7 and 8 on "Management Decision Making," chapter 20 on "Evaluating, Developing and Compensating," and chapter 23 on "Managerial Control." These chapters contain a variety of techniques for the management audit of business organizations.

Time-and-Motion Studies

DESCRIPTION

Time-and-motion studies refer to those methods that attempt to describe the use of time by program staff and administrators in relation to the activities in which they are involved. Information in these studies may be obtained from samples of program activity during selected periods; it might also contain reports by staff members on written forms, observations of and interviews with the staff, and the relationship of descriptions of actual staff activity to planned staff functions. The purposes of these methods are to specify the total time devoted by staff to program activities, to locate the uses of staff time that were not anticipated, and to recommend reallocations of staff time to those activities that might be more directly related to the potential achievement of program goals.

These studies are typically conducted by auditors, particularly administrative auditors (or management analysts) and cost accountants, who combine time-and-motion studies with studies of cost (see reference below by Elkin). Experts in the use of these methods attempt to obtain accurate information centered on time as the unit of measurement. Although time can be measured accurately by the use of a stopwatch in combination with observations of staff activity, many of these studies do not require such precise documentation to obtain an overall perspective of what time is devoted to what activity. Typically, self-reports by staff, over selected representative periods, are the primary data obtained. Thus, the procedures used are relatively inexpensive when self-reports are used. In addition, for large, complex programs, the costs can be reduced by using sampling methods (see references included in survey techniques in this chapter). For example, to describe the use of time during a given month, two weeks may be randomly selected. Following that selection, two half-day periods from each week may be chosen. Then, on those designated half days, staff may complete questionnaires on the way in which their time is spent on an hourly basis. Of course, the sampling and the unit of time selected vary depending upon the complexity and diversity of the program. Nevertheless, reasonably reliable information can be obtained within a short period at minimal costs.

USES

Time-and-motion studies are used primarily to describe the time devoted to program efforts. They are also useful as an indication of program efficiency with respect to time. The auditor may locate duplications of effort or excessive time spent on activities that may not be related to program goals.

These studies can be used for all stages of program development. In fact, as indicated earlier, the way in which staff time is allocated may give an indication of the stage of development toward which a program is moving. Moreover, a time-and-motion study may reveal whether a program is devoting necessary manpower to specified goals for its current stage of development. For example, a great deal of staff activity devoted to the recruitment of new staff when the program has already achieved that particular objective could be viewed as inefficient if the program is in the contact stage of development.

BIBLIOGRAPHY

Elkin, Robert. "Analyzing Time, Costs, and Operations in a Voluntary Children's Institution and Agency." Project on Cost Analysis in Children's Institutions, North Building, U. S. Department of Health, Education, and Welfare, Washington, D.C., September 1965, pp. 27–39.

This is a study of a children's institution that uses a cost-analysis procedure recommended by the Child Welfare League of America. Included in the study is a section devoted to the use of time by personnel and the percentage of that time directed to the care and treatment of individual children.

Epstein, Irwin, and Tripodi, Tony. *Research Techniques for Program Planning, Monitoring and Evaluation*. New York: Columbia University Press, 1977.

Chapter 7 presents principles for devising forms for measuring amounts and kinds of staff activities.

Hill, John G. "Cost Analysis of Social Work Service." In *Social Work Research,* edited by Norman A. Polansky, pp. 238–42. Chicago: The University of Chicago Press, 1960.

In the pages designated above, the author discusses the notion of time sampling as used in a study of social services in Philadelphia.

Terry, George R. *Principles of Management.*

6th ed. Homewood, Ill.: Richard D. Irwin, 1972.

Chapter 26, "Time Use, Cost and Budgetary Controlling," pp. 603–10, discusses the use of time and its control by management.

SOCIAL-RESEARCH STRATEGIES

Experiments

DESCRIPTION

The purpose of *experiments* is to provide evidence whether program efforts are related causally to the accomplishment of program goals. Logical procedures are employed for setting up experimental arrangements and the collection of data such that inferences can be made about the effects of the program. In a frequently used model of experimentation, the *classical experimental design*, objectives of the program and the means to accomplish those objectives are specified and standardized. Criterion variables considered relevant to the effects of a program are defined precisely so they can be measured. The target population is determined, and a representative sample of that population is secured through probability sampling techniques. The members of the sample are assigned randomly to experimental (one or more groups that receive program efforts) and control groups (one or more groups that are similar to the experimental group with respect to all relevant characteristics except that they do not receive efforts of the program or efforts from other programs that are similar). Finally, the groups are measured before and after program intervention and compared, with respect to change, on the criterion variables.

The data used in experiments may be obtained from questionnaires, observations of behavior, self-reports, interviews, tests, ratings, and so forth. The information gathered is for the purpose of showing change that can be attributed primarily to the program: for example, the procurement of jobs by welfare recipients, completion of school, reduction of physical and mental symptoms of disturbance, changes in attitudes, and so forth.

Experimentalists are those persons who are expert in the formulation and application of experimental methods. Those experts usually have secured their training in experimental methods in sociology or psychology and/or in applied statistical and biostatistical methods. The problems that must be solved by the experimenter, in conjunction with program personnel, include specifying program intervention presumably related to program effects, delineating who or what is to receive program intervention and for what period, the inclusion of adequate control groups, and the specification of measurable variables that provide valid and reliable information pertaining to those effects that could be attributed to the program being evaluated.

Experimentalists, in many instances, cannot use the classical experimental design because ideal experimental arrangements are not possible or practical. Therefore, those experts may devise quasi-experiments or approximations to experiments. For example, instead of a control group as used in the classical experimental design, comparative groups such as the following may be used:

1. A group similar to the experimental group on many relevant variables, selected after the experimental group has received program intervention
2. A group similar to the experimental group that receives less frequent program efforts rather than no program intervention
3. A group similar to the experimental group that receives a routine, traditional intervention in contrast to the experimental group, which also receives the routine, traditional intervention, as well as an additional, innovative intervention
4. The experimental group used as its own control, with comparisons made on criterion measures before and after program intervention

In approximations to experiments there is less certainty of the knowledge obtained than in true experiments, but useful evidence pertaining to cause-effect assertions can be gathered. In the references below by Herbert Hyman et al. and Donald Campbell and Julian Stanley, a variety of experiments and approximations to experiments are discussed with respect to the certainty of knowledge that can be produced. Moreover, Irwin Epstein and Tony Tripodi present experimental designs that can be applied by administrative staff in social agencies.

Experiments used to evaluate comprehensive social programs involve extensive periods for their execution and analysis. More rigor is included than in other research procedures, and this means that program goals and operations must be relatively standardized. In addition, after the program intervention is terminated, follow-up information on program beneficiaries should be obtained to determine whether observed changes are temporary or long-lasting. Although comprehensive program experiments are costly, the knowledge produced from experiments may not be obtainable by any other means.

USES

Experiments and quasi-experiments are used primarily for evaluating the effects of programs in the implementation stage. For example, a program on reading disability might be evaluated with respect to the reduction of reading disabilities in a group that receives program intervention, as compared to a group that has reading disabilities but does not receive any program efforts. If reading disabilities are reduced more frequently in the experimental group and if it can be demonstrated that the possible effects of other variables are controlled, it might be inferred that the program is effective with respect to the criterion of the reduction of reading disabilities.

Experiments can also be employed for other stages of development. For example, in the program-contact stage, two or more different methods for involving program recipients may be compared with a control group to determine which methods are effective and which method is the most efficient in terms of greater effectiveness for its efforts. Or the same method may be employed, but using two or more comparison groups, to determine the extent to which intensity of contacts (e.g., number of interviews with potential program participants) yields similar or greater results. Thus, experiments can be used to determine the relative efficiency of program efforts for any of the three stages of development. They deal primarily with effects, but they can be used to indicate the relative efficiency of different amounts and kinds of program effort. They are not used for determining whether program efforts have been achieved.

BIBLIOGRAPHY

Campbell, Donald T., and Stanley, Julian C. "Experimental and Quasi-experimental Designs for Research on Teaching." In *Handbook of Research on Teaching,* edited by N. A. Gage, pp. 171–246. Chicago: Rand McNally and Co., 1963.

This is a classic treatise on principles of control in experimentation. A variety of experimental designs with their advantages and disadvantages is presented. Examples are from education, but the principles of experimentation also apply to social programs in health and welfare.

Epstein, Irwin, and Tripodi, Tony. *Research Techniques for Program Planning, Monitoring and Evaluation*. New York: Columbia University Press, 1977.

The last four chapters specify how to employ the following designs in program evaluation: interrupted time series, replicated cross sectional designs, comparative designs, and crossover designs.

Hyman, Herbert H.; Wright, Charles R.; and Hopkins, Terence K. *Applications of Methods of Evaluation*. Berkeley and Los Angeles: University of California Press, 1962.

Four evaluative research studies of The Encampment for Citizenship, a social program, are presented. In Part I on "Principles of Evaluation," pp. 3–85, the authors discuss experimental design and approximations to experimental design they employed in their studies. Their discussion of evaluation is excellent.

Riecken, Henry W., and Boruch, Robert F., eds. *Social Experimentation: A Method for Planning and Evaluating Social Intervention*. New York: Academic Press, 1974.

This is an excellent textbook; it provides specific procedures, examples, problems, and prospects in devising and carrying out social experiments.

Suchman, Edward A. *Evaluative Research: Principles and Practice in Public Service and*

Social Action Programs. New York: Russell Sage Foundation, 1967.

This is a text on evaluative research that includes a variety of examples from the field of public health. Experimental methods are emphasized and clarified in chapter 5, "The Conduct of Evaluative Research"; chapter 6, "The Evaluative Research Design"; and chapter 7, "The Measurement of Effects."

Weiss, Carol H. *Evaluation Research.* Englewood Cliffs, N. J., Prentice-Hall, 1972.

A well-written excellent introduction to experiments and quasi-experiments is provided in chapter 4.

Surveys

DESCRIPTION

Survey methods are those methods that aim to yield facts descriptive of a social program. Included among these facts are the accurate description of the target population (i.e., that population a program intends to benefit) with respect to attitudes, opinions, and reported changes in behavior. In addition to the descriptive function of the accumulation of accurate facts and statements of opinion representative of the target population, surveys may also have an explanatory function, which may be accomplished by such devices as the analysis of many variables simultaneously, as in multivariate analysis (see reference by Hyman below), or by surveys of comparative groups, as in quasi-experiments or approximations to experiments. For example, those who have heart disease are compared with those who do not, with respect to cigarette smoking and other kinds of habits and characteristics, in an effort to locate possible causal connections between other factors and heart disease.

A survey typically involves the designation of a target population; the selection of a representative sample from that population, using techniques of probability sampling (see reference below by Babbie); the collection of data, primarily from constructed questionnaires or interview schedules; the use of procedures to verify the accuracy of the accumulated information and to minimize response and interviewer biases; and the processing and analysis of data. Analyses are conducted in relation to the objectives of the survey, the completion of information, and available techniques of data processing.

Experts in survey techniques are usually social scientists, such as sociologists or social psychologists with special training in survey methods, public opinion and market research specialists, or epidemiologists and biostatisticians who have had their training in public health and mathematics or statistics. In addition, they may be attached to reputable survey-research centers within universities such as Michigan, Columbia, and Chicago, or in private business such as the Gallup organization.

The survey is a flexible technique, and it can be

adapted to fit varying cost budgets. It can provide simple descriptive facts more quickly than experiments, and it is less costly than experiments when it is used to provide evidence for hypotheses related to social programs. However, although representative samples are more often obtained in surveys than in experiments, experiments have greater degrees of control for ruling out the influence of variables other than program efforts that could be responsible for observed changes in program beneficiaries. The most efficient aspect of surveys is the use of sampling procedures. Results from a sample can be used to generalize to the total target population, and the expert use of this procedure can result in reduced costs. Nevertheless, a good survey involves necessary expenses: the sample selection; the construction and pretesting of appropriate interview schedules; the training and hiring of interviewers; data processing; and so forth. Depending upon the scope and desired accuracy of the survey, some costs can be reduced—for example, by using program staff as interviewers.

USES

Survey techniques can be used in all stages of program development. During the initiation of a program, survey techniques can be used to determine the need for the program on the part of people in designated communities, the incidence and prevalence of disease, low literacy rates, malnutrition, inadequate housing, and so forth.

In the program-contact stage, survey methods can be used to describe the extent to which program personnel are making efforts to involve program beneficiaries. Moreover, the effectiveness of these efforts can be determined. For example, the proportion of the target population contacted by the program can be estimated and related to the program goals. Survey techniques can be combined with cost-analytic techniques and time-and-motion studies to form estimates of the program's efficiency.

Survey methods can be used as approximations to experiments to provide evidence that bears on the total effectiveness of the social program. For example, data such as the percentage of the target population contacted, processed through a job-training program, and placed in jobs might be critical information for evaluating the effectiveness of the job-training program.

BIBLIOGRAPHY

Babbie, Earl R. *Survey Research Methods,* pp. 73–129. Belmont, Calif.: Wadsworth Publishing Company, 1973.

A variety of sampling designs employed in survey design and analysis are presented. Probability sampling theory is also introduced.

Epstein, Irwin, and Tripodi, Tony. *Research Techniques for Program Planning, Monitoring and Evaluation.* New York: Columbia University Press, 1977.

Chapters 2 and 3 contain principles for constructing questionnaires and interview schedules, and chapter 8 includes a discussion of elementary sampling concepts.

Glock, Charles Y., ed. *Survey Research in the Social Sciences.* New York: Russell Sage Foundation, 1967.

A collection of articles is presented on the uses of survey research in a variety of disciplines. In particular, these articles are recommended: "Education and Survey Research," by Martin Trow, pp. 315–76; "The Survey Method in Social Work: Past, Present, and Potential," by Fred Massarika, pp. 377–422; and "The Survey Method Applied to Public Health and Medicine," by Edward A. Suchman, pp. 423–519.

Hayes, Samuel P., Jr. *Evaluating Development Projects.* 2nd ed. reprinted, 116 pp. Belgium: UNESCO, 1967.

This is an excellent handbook that incorporates survey methods and other research methods for evaluating social development projects in a variety of countries. The principles discussed are applicable to the formation of social programs in a variety of substantive areas such as agriculture, housing, education, and disease control.

Hyman, Herbert. *Survey Design and Analysis.* Glencoe, Ill.: The Free Press, 1957.

Principles and procedures for surveys are presented concisely and logically. Descriptions of actual studies with the questionnaires that were used and principles of data analysis are also included. Chapters 1 and 2 provide the reader with perspectives adopted by the survey analyst, and chapters 8 and 9 are excellent in their discussions of the use of survey findings for public policy and for applied purposes such as programmatic evaluations.

Moser, C. A. *Survey Methods in Social Investigation.* London: Heinemann Educational Books, Ltd., 1965.

This is a basic book that covers all aspects of a survey, from the definition of the population and sample design to the construction and analysis of questionnaires and interviews.

Case Study

DESCRIPTION

The *case-study strategy* has as its purpose the detailed description of a social program as it unfolds in its process of development. It employs both qualitative and quantitative data in an effort to develop hypotheses and new ideas for explaining the progress or lack of progress in program development. Among the methods used are participant observation, informal interviews, and methods of group analysis such as sociometric devices and content analyses of written documents.

Experts in this technique are social scientists: the

social psychologist for the study of groups; the sociologist for the study of organizations and communities; the anthropologist for the study of cultural and subcultural differences; and the psychologist for the study of individuals. An expert in this technique attempts to accumulate as much information as possible; then he uses that information in relation to a conceptual scheme he develops for generating ideas. For example, a sociologist may be hired to study a social program that includes a group-living situation for the purpose of increasing the adjustment of delinquent boys. The expert may seek to participate in the group-living situation as an observer, but without responsibility for program operations. He reviews official policies, documents, and rules; and he may live with the group to increase his awareness from their perspective. He talks with people connected with the program and with other organizations that might be closely related to the program. Following this, he may develop a conceptual scheme from his experience in the group and from his previous experiences and knowledge of groups and organizations. Quantitative data are then collected with respect to group behavior and the way in which the program attempts to influence it. That information is used for developing ideas and hypotheses about future program directions, particularly its relation to organizations concerned with delinquency and its influence on community adjustment through the use of living groups. Moreover, if problems are discovered in the group program, recommendations might be made for their solution.

A detailed case study takes time. However, a

small-sized research staff may be sufficient. Thus, the costs involved are primarily those for manpower, possibly tape-recording equipment and other clerical devices, and data processing and report writing. Costs are minimal when case-study experts give a few training sessions to staff in selected methods, such as recording procedures and content analysis (see reference below by Riley). The staff, in turn, uses those methods routinely.

USES

Case study strategy may be particularly helpful for developing programs where there is difficulty in specifying objectives and in selecting programmatic means to accomplish those objectives. Furthermore, some of the methods employed in case studies, as indicated above, may be used by program staff. For example, each staff person may keep a diary of what activities he or she is engaged in, for what reasons, and with what success. Periodically, the contents of those diaries are reviewed to discover possible strategies that could be used by all staff members more consistently.

The case-study approach can also be used to pinpoint potential problems in program operations. For example, a case study might reveal that the primary problem in not being able to contact program beneficiaries who are representative of the "intended target population" is that there are differences of opinion among staff persons, and between staff and administration, with respect to who should be contacted.

Information from the case study is principally used for

an evaluation of program efforts with respect to the nature and quantity of staff activities and the extent to which staff efforts are related to program goals as perceived by different staff members. However, indirect information can be gathered that bears on possible reasons for program ineffectiveness and inefficiency: location of staff conflicts, different vested interests, and so forth.

BIBLIOGRAPHY

Bloom, Bernard L. "The Evaluation of Primary Prevention Programs." In *Comprehensive Mental Health,* edited by Leigh M. Roberts, Norman S. Greenfield, and Milton H. Miller, pp. 117–36. Madison, Wisc.: The University of Wisconsin Press, 1968.

Different types of evaluation are discussed, and guideline questions are presented for mental-health program directors. Of particular import is the brief discussion pertaining to the use of a program diary for describing mental-health programs.

Bolgar, Hedda. "The Case Study Method." In *Handbook of Clinical Psychology,* edited by Benjamin B. Wolman, pp. 28–39. New York: McGraw-Hill Book Company, 1965.

The nature of the case-study approach as used for the discovery and generation of hypotheses in clinical research is discussed.

Epstein, Irwin, and Tripodi, Tony. *Research*

Techniques for Program Planning, Monitoring and Evaluation. New York: Columbia University Press, 1977.

Chapter 5 discusses the use of observational techniques for program planning. Such techniques can also be applied for evaluative purposes, since the basic principles of observation are clearly described.

McCall, George J., and Simmons, J. L., eds. *Issues in Participant Observation.* Reading, Mass.: Addison-Wesley, 1969.

This is a book of readings on the method of participant observation. Recommended articles are "Some Methodological Problems of Field Studies," by Morris Zelditch, Jr., pp. 5–18; "Data Quality Control in Participant Observation," by George J. McCall, pp. 128–41; "Problems of Inference and Proof in Participant Observation," by Howard S. Becker, pp. 245–57; and "A Comparison of Participant Observation and Survey Data," by Arthur J. Vidich and Gilbert Shapiro, pp. 295–302.

Riley, Matilda White. *Sociological Research: A Case Approach.* New York: Harcourt, Brace & World, 1963.

This is a textbook in research methods for sociologists. The sections on "Descriptive Case Studies," pp. 32–77; "Questioning Compared with Observation," pp. 132–93; and "Uses of Available Data," pp. 194–255, deal with a variety of methods used in case studies: sociometric procedures, observations, interviews, content analysis, and so forth. Advantages and disadvantages of the methods are reviewed in their applications to actual studies.

COST-ANALYTIC STRATEGIES

General Accounting

DESCRIPTION

General accounting refers to the program's system for keeping track of program costs, including payroll, purchasing, and so forth. An audit or review of general-accounting procedures is conducted, typically, by an auditor or an experienced accountant versed in the operations of programs similar to the one being reviewed. The auditor attempts to verify the accuracy of the recorded financial status of the program. In addition, he or she seeks to determine whether the general-accounting system used by the program is sufficiently monitored by relevant staff to determine whether the assets of the program are safeguarded, the accuracy and reliability of accounting data are maintained, and the prescribed managerial and operating procedures are followed. The auditor locates written policies regarding the accounting procedures, and he or she may interview those staff persons who perform accounting functions to obtain an overview of the flow of information concerning the program's cost procedures and to determine whether there are mechanisms for internal verification of the accuracy of those procedures. The auditor then may look at the accounting books that are maintained and make a judgment about whether those books (such as a cash and in-kind receipts journal) are in accordance with acceptable general-accounting procedures. Finally, he or she reviews the accounts for accuracy and consistency.

The knowledge obtained by an audit of general accounting consists of verification of the program's system and recommendations for improving the dependability of the program's accounting procedures. The costs involved are primarily the salaries of one or more auditors for a brief period, perhaps one or two weeks. However, the costs obviously depend upon the scope and complexity of the program's general-accounting procedures and the extent to which those procedures are developed. Assistance initially in setting up accounting procedures, for example, may be less costly than later finding an error in the system and recommending a more dependable, but different, system of accounting.

USES

General-accounting audits are especially useful for determining the extent to which a social program administrator has made efforts to establish an effective and efficient system of accounting in the initiation stage of program development.

A good accounting system is necessary for the development of reliable cost information that can be used for cost accounting and performance budgeting in the contact stage. Moreover, cost-benefit and cost-effectiveness analyses, which are primarily employed in the implementation stage of development, rely on a good accounting of program costs.

BIBLIOGRAPHY

Charnes, Abraham; Colantoni, Claude S.; Cooper, William W.; and Kortanek, K. O. "Economic, Social and Enterprise Accounting and Mathematical Models." In *Accounting for Social Goals,* edited by John L. Livingstone and Sanford C. Gunn, pp. 230–59. New York: Harper and Row, 1974.

The application of mathematical models for describing various aspects of accounting is presented. Of particular interest is a discussion of input-output analysis and of accounting spread sheets.

Hill, John G. "Cost Analysis of Social Work Service." In *Social Work Research,* edited by Norman A. Polansky, pp. 223–46. Chicago: The University of Chicago Press, 1960.

Distinctions between general accounting and cost accounting are discussed, and examples of accounting principles for health and welfare agencies are presented.

Kaplan, Robert S. "Management Accounting in Hospitals: A Case Study." In *Accounting for Social Goals,* edited by John L. Livingstone and Sanford C. Gunn, pp. 131–48. New York: Harper and Row, 1974.

This case illustration of an accounting system stresses the relationship between management decision making and budgeting systems employed in general accounting.

Terry, George R. *Principles of Management.* 6th ed. Homewood, Ill.: Richard D. Irwin, 1972.

This is a comprehensive text on management principles. Chapter 23 on "Managerial Controlling" and chapter 24 on "Overall Managerial Controls and Audits" are essential sources for background information on principles of general accounting as used in business organizations. The principles discussed are applicable to the financial and general accounting operations of social programs.

.

Cost Accounting

DESCRIPTION

The purpose of *cost accounting* is to relate program costs to program outputs. *Outputs* are those program actions that are measurable: number of children placed in adoption, number of therapy interviews, number of health examinations, and so forth. The same principles as those in general accounting are used, but, in addition, cost accounting produces unit-cost figures as a basis for analyzing, budgeting, and allocating resources. The cost accountant is an expert in the use of accounting methods, agency forms, and, oftentimes, in program planning. He reviews general- and social-accounting records similarly to the auditor. He devises categories of unit costs for program service; then he relates them to the general- and social-accounting data, as well as to information from time-and-motion studies, so he can describe how much money and time are expended for what kinds of staff activities in relation to specified program objectives. For example, statements such as the following might be made: X funds were expended for using Y man-hours to recruit Z persons to participate in the social program. Thus, the knowledge from cost accounting is that of simple facts relating program resources to program outputs.

Among the objectives of cost accounting are the improvement of program budgeting and the procurement of information for determining program-service priorities as a function of costs. An extension of cost accounting is program budgeting, which organizes cost data for use in assessing alternative program actions in relation to their cost and utility. Program budgeting, which emphasizes program objectives and possible alternatives, is increasingly being employed by large organizations in an attempt to improve program planning within restricted budgets. John Pfeiffer (see reference below) gives an excellent introduction to program budgeting and its possible applications to education.

Cost-accounting and program-budgeting strategies are difficult to employ when the program objectives are unspecified or when the categories of unit cost are ambiguous. Although information relating costs to program outputs can be readily obtained, reliable data relating program objectives to costs and outputs are not easily produced. Thus, the costs for using these strategies increase in relation to the ambiguity and imprecision of program objectives and program outputs related to those objectives. In addition, since cost accounting depends upon an adequate general-accounting system, the costs would decrease in relation to the adequacy of the general-accounting system used by the program.

USES

Cost accounting is used primarily for the evaluation of program efficiency in the program-contact stage. For example, a program that intends to give health examinations to a designated population may be evaluated with respect to the relative costs involved in completing examinations in different geographical locations. Moreover, different parts of the examination may be administered by physicians, nurses, nonprofessionals, and so on; the cost and utility of the use of different professionals for administering different aspects of the program (such as reading an eye chart, weighing the patient, taking a social history, etc.) might be assessed.

The information yielded by cost-accounting studies may be used to initiate different procedures in a social program in relation to general accounting and the redistribution of program efforts. Moreover, cost accounting provides basic data used for evaluating the effectiveness and efficiency of social programs by such strategies as cost-benefit analysis (which is discussed subsequently).

BIBLIOGRAPHY

Elkin, Robert. "Analyzing Time, Costs, and Operations in a Voluntary Children's Institution and Agency." Project on Cost Analysis in Children's Institutions, North Building, U. S. Department of Health, Education, and Welfare, Washington, D.C., September 1965, pp. 27–39.

This study employs a variety of cost-accounting procedures as recommended by the Child Welfare League of America.

Hill, John C. "Cost Analysis of Social Work Service." In *Social Work Research,* edited by Norman A. Polansky, pp. 223–46. Chicago: The University of Chicago Press, 1960.

Principles of cost accounting are discussed for social-welfare organizations. They are also applicable to health and education programs.

Hoffenberg, Marvin. "Group Decisions and the Allocation of Social Resources." In *Accounting*

for Social Goals, edited by John A. Livingstone and Sanford C. Gunn, pp. 35–38. New
York: Harper and Row, 1974.

Advantages of planning-programming-
budgeting systems and the contributions of
goal analyses are presented.

Pfeiffer, John. *New Look at Education: Systems
Analysis in Our Schools and Colleges,* Poughkeepsie, N. Y.: Odyssey Press, 1968.

In chapter 2, the author gives an introduction to program budgeting and other methods
used for making program decisions.

Cost-Benefit Analysis

DESCRIPTION

Cost-benefit analysis is a strategy for evaluating the
relative effectiveness of alternative programs, or aspects
of programs, in terms of cost. Its purpose is to ascertain
the relationship of required resources (costs) to the
attainment of specified goals (benefits). This type of
analysis is geared to answering questions such as which of
a number of possible income-maintenance programs will
result in optimal benefits under any given allocation of
resources (see reference below by Levine). Essential
elements in cost-benefit analysis are costs (financial costs
of manpower and other resources), benefits (whether
desired objectives have been achieved, and the monetary
value that can be ascribed to such achievements), and the

specification of objectives, goals, and values. As is true in cost accounting, program inputs are first related to program outputs or staff actions; program outputs are then related to the results of those actions. The cost-benefit analyst attempts to translate criteria of goal achievement into monetary units, to make an appraisal of the economic benefits of the program relative to the costs of program resources and activities. For example, the benefits from a program for training welfare recipients for jobs might be reflected in the extent to which the recipients received jobs, and the money thus saved from welfare-department expenditures, as well as the money contributed to society through taxes and so forth. In the comparison of two programs, which for the sake of illustration are assumed to be similar in all respects except costs and benefits, that program which has a greater benefit-to-cost ratio would be regarded as the most efficient.

Cost-benefit analyses are conducted by economists, systems engineers, and program planners who have developed expertise in the technique. Cost-benefit analysts use accounting methods and economic methods of analysis, along with graphic and tabular presentations to represent mathematical units of relationship. They attempt to convert social indicators of program objectives into economic indices or into other indices that could be measured and translated into economic terms. Data are gathered from forms for recording program statistics, general- and cost-accounting records, social-accounting records, and so forth.

The knowledge produced is in the form of descriptive

facts relating costs to benefits. However, such knowledge is valid only insofar as the indicators of "benefits" can be translated into monetary units. Some benefits may not be registerable in monetary equivalents, or, just as problematic, the assigned economic value may be purely arbitrary. The costs of such analyses are greater than those for cost accounting, because more variables are related. But the potential knowledge derived, when the indicators of "benefits" appear to be accurately reflected in monetary units, is much more useful for making decisions about program alternatives. In fact, a key ingredient in planning is the consideration of alternative uses and amounts of program resources (costs) to achieve specified benefits. Such cost-benefit planning is more likely to lead to efficient alternatives than is cost accounting.

USES

Cost-benefit analyses are employed primarily to evaluate the efficiency and relative effectiveness of social programs in the implementation stage of development. As indicated above, analyses are more immediately useful for programs having objectives that can be readily translated into economic units (getting off the welfare rolls, receiving jobs at given wages, etc.).

The product of cost-benefit analyses might also contain recommendations for choosing among various alternative strategies for allocating program resources, that is, a rationale is provided for maintaining or shifting program efforts in relation to costs and benefits.

In the reference below by Abraham Levine, a cost-benefit analysis of a government job-retraining program is described. Although benefit-cost ratios were produced with respect to estimated earnings and program costs, psychological and sociological benefits were ignored because they could not be easily quantified into monetary units. This deficiency has led different analysts to use cost-effectiveness analysis, which is discussed in the next section of this chapter.

BIBLIOGRAPHY

Alkin, Marvin C. "Evaluating the Cost-Effective-
    ness of Instructional Programs." Center for the
    Study of Evaluation of Instructional Programs,
    University of California, Los Angeles,
    California, 1969
        Distinctions between cost-benefit analysis
    and cost-effectiveness evaluation are made,
    and an approach is presented for evaluating
    instructional programs in education.
Glaser, Daniel. *Routinizing Evaluation: Getting
    Feedback on Effectiveness of Crime and
    Delinquency Programs.* DHEW Publication
    No. (HSM) 73-9123. Rockville, Md.: National
    Institute of Mental Health, 1973.
        In chapter 4 various approaches for con-
    sidering cost-benefit relationships for correc-
    tional institutions are clearly presented.
Levine, Abraham S. "Cost-Benefit Analysis and

Social Welfare: An Exploration of Possible Applications." *Welfare in Review* 4, no. 2 (February 1966): 1–11.

Principles of cost-benefit analysis are discussed and applied to social welfare. For illustrative purposes, an actual study of unemployment is presented.

Neenan, William B. *Normative Evaluation of a Public Health Program.* 74 pp. Ann Arbor, Mich.: Institute of Public Administration, The University of Michigan, 1967.

This is a cost-benefit analysis of the Michigan Department of Public Health's X-ray tuberculosis-control program. Economic criteria are presented and applied, and detailed findings of the study are included.

Rothenberg, Jerome. "Cost-Benefit Analysis: A Methodological Exposition." In *Handbook of Evaluation Research.* Vol. 2, pp. 55–58. Edited by Marcia Guttentag and Elmer L. Struening, Beverly Hills, Calif.: Sage Publications, 1975.

Basic principles of economics necessary for cost-benefit analyses are presented, and methodological issues in the application of cost-benefit analyses are discussed.

Cost-Effectiveness Analysis

DESCRIPTION

Whereas cost-benefit analysis attempts to relate program costs to the results of program activities in terms of monetary units, *cost-effectiveness analysis* relates program costs to program results (outcomes) without translating outcomes into economic indicators. The purpose of cost-effectiveness analysis is to gauge the relative efficiency of the costs of alternative program inputs with respect to the accomplishment of specified objectives. The objectives might be fixed, while the costs of program input vary. For example, the fixed objective might be the attainment of a nondelinquency rate of 90 per cent for a target population of delinquent youth. Two alternative programs with varying costs may both result in a nondelinquency rate of 90 per cent. That program which entails the lower costs would be regarded as the more efficient program. Thus, the essence of cost-effectiveness analysis is the determination of the minimum costs necessary to produce a given outcome.

Cost-effectiveness analysis is a strategy that involves a combination of social-research and cost-accounting methods. Hence, the expert's background may be similar to that of social researchers (experimentalists or survey analysts) and/or to cost analysts (cost-benefit or cost-accounting analysts).

The knowledge produced is, typically, descriptive facts: group therapy for a designated population is cheaper than individual therapy in achieving a 70 per cent rate of reduction in psychological symptoms; a classroom size of twenty involves less per pupil cost than one of ten for attaining a specified goal of reading improvement; and so forth.

Of course, this strategy is most easily applicable when outcomes can be specified and fixed. When outcomes are variable and costs are also variable, the analysis takes on the character of experimental or survey research, with costs regarded as one of the independent variables that could lead to program results. For example, in the reference below, Marvin Alkin discusses a model for cost-effectiveness analysis in instructional programs. He regards student inputs, financial inputs, descriptive characteristics of students and school personnel, and features of external systems in the environment as independent variables that could lead to, or be associated with, program outcomes such as cognitive and noncognitive changes in students.

If program objectives are fixed and easily attained, a cost-effectiveness analysis is not too expensive for comparing the relative costs of different approaches. In such situations, the strategy is less costly than cost-benefit analysis, particularly when the criteria for program outcomes are sociological or psychological, as opposed to economic. However, if a variety of program input and outcome measures are used, the costs would exceed those typically required for surveys and experiments.

USES

Cost-effectiveness analysis is most useful as a device for assessing the relative efficiency of alternative programs, or aspects of programs, in the implementation stage. However, if outcomes are interpreted broadly to include fixed objectives for achieving specified program goals, the strategy can be employed for all program stages. Answers might be provided to questions such as the following: what are the relative costs for recruiting X staff persons, involving Y program recipients, delivering Z services, and so forth.

Cost-effectiveness analysis might also provide information to administrators for making decisions about the distributions of costs that go into program efforts. Moreover, as in Alkin's model, the strategy can be used for determining relative efficiency as well as program effectiveness.

BIBLIOGRAPHY

Alkin, Marvin C. "Evaluating the Cost-Effectiveness of Instructional Programs." Los Angeles: Center for the Study of Evaluation of Instructional Programs, University of California, 1969.

A model is presented for the use of cost-effectiveness evaluation in instructional programs.

Levin, Henry M. "Cost-Effectiveness Analysis in Evaluation Research." In *Handbook of Evaluation Research*. Vol. 2, pp. 89–122. Edited by Marcia Guttentag and Elmer L. Struening. Beverly Hills, Calif.: Sage Publications, 1975.

Principles for measuring and comparing costs are presented and illustrated.

Levine, Abraham S. "Evaluating Program Effectiveness and Efficiency: Rationale and Description of Research in Progress." *Welfare in Review* 5, no. 2 (February 1967): 1–11.

A model is formulated for the comparative evaluation of social, educational, and vocational services in AFDC programs.

DIFFERENTIAL EVALUATION

In previous chapters we discussed stages of program development, evaluation objectives, and evaluation strategies. The purpose of this chapter is to tie these ideas together. In it we attempt to integrate previous content by connecting specific evaluation objectives with stages of program development and with suggested evaluation strategies.[1] We call this matching of evaluation objective, program stage, and evaluation strategy *differential evaluation*.

To facilitate differential evaluation we provide tables throughout the chapter that match appropriate evaluation strategies with questions concerning program effort, effectiveness, and efficiency, and with stages of program initiation, contact, and implementation. By identifying

---

[1] It must be stressed, however, that our proposed matchings are suggestive, rather than definitive, and that our major purpose is to refine further our conception of differential evaluation.

the current stage of program development and the most critical evaluation questions facing a program administrator, he or she can use these tables to locate the evaluation strategies that could best answer specific evaluation questions. Decisions about which evaluation strategies to choose should be based on knowledge of available evaluation resources and the costs of using these resources. These issues are discussed in the final chapter.

THE PROCESS OF DIFFERENTIAL EVALUATION

Evaluation is a management technique for providing feedback of information to program administrators. Under ideal conditions, it is a continuous process that may involve more than one systematic collection of data and the use of more than one evaluation strategy. Ultimately, social program evaluation seeks to compile information about achievements or failures in program implementation. However, achievement of overall program goals is often dependent on the success with which the problems of program initiation and contact have been managed. Some social programs never transcend the difficulties of dealing with these earlier developmental stages. In such programs, evaluation of program implementation alone would document the lack of ultimate program achievement but would say little about the reasons for this lack of achievement. Sometimes, external funding sources require routine evaluations before program implementation is even contemplated. Here again, an analysis of the effects of program interventions would be premature and relatively unproductive.

In attempting to make evaluation more relevant and responsive to program development, we are proposing the idea of differential evaluation. The process of differential evaluation involves delineating evaluation objectives that are appropriate to specific stages of program development and choosing evaluation strategies pertinent to these objectives. More precisely, a differential evaluation of a social program would involve the following:

1. Specification of long-range and immediate operating goals and the means to accomplish these goals
2. Determination of the current stage of program development and collection of information about problems in attaining goals of former or subsequent program stages
3. Delineation of an hierarchy of program objectives in terms of their importance to the program
4. Formulation of evaluation objectives relevant to important program objectives for the current stage(s) of program development
5. Selection of evaluation strategies that will provide information pertaining to evaluation objectives, within time and cost constraints of the social program and its sponsors
6. Review of information retrieved through evaluation

and translation into decisions about future program planning

7. Repetition of the foregoing steps as the program expands, contracts, or otherwise changes

The following sections of this chapter are illustrative of the application of differential evaluation to different kinds of social programs. The reader may choose to read through it from beginning to end to get a sense of the versatility of many evaluation strategies. To plan an evaluation, however, the reader might limit himself or herself to those sections pertaining to his or her program's particular stage of program development.

MATCHING EVALUATION QUESTIONS AND STRATEGIES

Program Initiation

EFFORTS

Table 1 includes four selected evaluation strategies and six evaluation questions of effort for the program-initiation stage. For the illustrative questions we posed, the evaluation strategies of time-and-motion study, administrative audit, general accounting, and case study were judged to be, in general, more appropriate than other strategies. In the same row as each evaluation question on the table, an "X" in the column for an evaluation strategy

Table 1   109

Selected Strategies for
Evaluation of Effort, Program Initiation

Evaluation Questions	Time-and-Motion Study	Administrative Audit	General Accounting	Case Study
1. How much time and activity are devoted to the recruitment of staff for the program?	X			
2. What is the extent and type of activity devoted to the location of resources and the procurement of program co-operation?	X			X
3. What is the extent of involvement in the development of personnel policies and practices and adequate accounting, bookkeeping, and data-collection procedures?		X	X	
4. What are the number and nature of activities devoted to the development of an operational plan, the review of existing programs of a similar nature, a review of the literature for alternative approaches, and interviews with persons who have experience in similar programs?		X		
5. To what extent are efforts made to define and locate the potential target population?	X	X		X
6. What efforts are focused on the learning of statutes, ordinances, and regulations relevant to the program?	X	X		

Note: An "X" indicates that the evaluation strategy in a designated column can be employed to answer the evaluation question in the same row.

indicates that the strategy can provide useful information for answering the evaluation question.[2] Hence, the strategies of administrative audit and general accounting are recommended as useful for answering question 3 ("What is the extent of involvement in the development of personnel policies and practices and adequate accounting, bookkeeping, and data-collection procedures?"); an administrative audit is regarded as most useful for answering question 4 ("What are the number and nature of activities devoted to the development of an operational plan, the review of existing programs of a similar nature, a review of the literature for alternative approaches, and interviews with persons who have experience in similar programs?").

Question 1 (Q_1) has the purpose of seeking information about programmatic efforts by administrators and sponsors to recruit staff. Obviously, programs need the necessary staff to be operational; moreover, in many programs, there is difficulty in hiring staff that are adequately trained to carry out their proposed functions. If there is little success in hiring staff, a time-and-motion study could be done of administrators and/or sponsors. For example, some administrators may claim they are unable to recruit qualified staff from minority groups; a time-and-motion study might reveal how much time and what activities actually were devoted to such recruiting. If very little time is expended compared to recruitment efforts of other programs that have successfully recruited

---

[2] The same procedure for matching evaluation strategies and evaluation questions will be followed for tables 2–9.

minority-group members, a decision could be made to increase those efforts.

In the initiation stage of a social program, the location of resources and the procurement of cooperation are vital. Q_2 intends to seek whether efforts at cooperation were made among members within a staff as well as between staffs of different community programs. Important community leaders and agencies may aid or impede progress in program development. For example, cooperation of the police in an antidelinquency program located in a high delinquency area is important. Trust and cooperation between the program staff and the police may lead to appropriate referrals and program facilitation; a lack of cooperation may lead to premature detention and lockup for juveniles involved in the program. Time-and-motion studies can provide information about the amount of effort expended, but they may not be able to locate potential sources of conflict that hinder the program. If the staff appears to have difficulty in securing the cooperation necessary for the initiation of the program, it may be advisable to employ a case-study approach. An independent observer may examine the program ideology and the way in which staff interacts with community representatives; this process of observation may lead to the location of potential conflict and to hypotheses regarding the advantages and disadvantages of that conflict for program development.

The administrative audit and general-accounting procedures should be employed to answer Q_3. A social program must set up adequate procedures for making payments and keeping a record of them; it should have an accurate, yet efficient, accounting system. Moreover, the program administration should develop and implement fair personnel procedures, with appropriate grievance and appeal mechanisms for staff. An administrative audit is especially useful for programs that appear to have diffuse and ambiguous policies regarding personnel practices and information-gathering devices. The auditor may locate the management problems and make recommendations for clear and efficient policies that are, of course, in compliance with existing laws, statutes, ordinances, and governmental restrictions. It should be emphasized that good record-keeping systems need to be established in the initiation stage of a program, for subsequent stages of program development and program evaluations, such as cost accounting and cost-effectiveness analysis, rely on adequate records.

Q_4 is concerned with the specific hypotheses, strategies, and rationale for the social program. It is based on the assumption that the implementation of a social program is an operationalization of one or more ideas. Hence, the essence of Q_4 is that it seeks to ascertain what knowledge and planning ideas are used and available for staff and administration. The administrative audit is based on a review of available program documents, interviews with administrators and staff, and a review of similar programs and ideas.

Social programs provide services or technologies to selected target populations. In the initiation of many programs, it is often assumed that a population designated as being in need will actually participate in social programs; but this may or may not be true. Q_5 has the intent of determining whether a program staff has attempted to locate a group of persons who might participate in their program. The program administration should be able to estimate the size of the population, specify important population characteristics, such as age and income distribution, indicate referral sources, and provide some estimate of the likelihood that persons in the target population will participate. The administrative audit focuses on a review of administrative documents that indicate whether *any* efforts have been devoted to locating the target population; the time-and-motion study would be useful in determining the relative times devoted to these activities in comparison with other administrative activities. A case-study approach is more costly and time consuming, but it may be employed if there are difficulties in locating a target population. An observer may talk with representatives of the target population and may develop some insights about whether there is a target population that can be reached by the program. For example, young children may be in need of information about sex, but their parents may not allow them to participate in a program. As a result of a case study, it might be inferred that the target population should have included parents and their children, rather than being restricted to children only.

An administrator must be aware of statutes, ordinances, and regulations that influence his or her program. If a program is sponsored by the federal government, the administrator must see to it that his or her program complies with governmental regulations; however, the administrator first needs to know what those regulations are. Both the administrative audit and the time-and-motion study can be employed to answer Q_6. It is recommended that the time-and-motion study be used only if it is known that efforts have been made, but the administration does not have sufficient knowledge about them. Then it could be determined if more time should be devoted to those efforts; or it might be inferred, along with information from an administrative audit, that the administration simply is not competent to pursue that information.

EFFECTIVENESS

The administrative audit is that strategy which can be most easily used for evaluating effectiveness of program efforts in the initiation stage. (See table 2.) A review of personnel files and brief interviews with a program's administrative staff will provide answers to Q_1; the number of filled positions and the relationship of that to the recruiting efforts expended are easily attainable. Questions regarding the perception of community residents (Q_2) are much more difficult to answer by means of the administrative audit; in fact, the audit may reveal only whether the program staff has the information in terms of survey results, census statistics, written testimonials, or other documents. Program staff may also be queried regarding their beliefs of the extent to which community residents might participate in the program, but that information may be tinged with programmatic hopes, expectations, biases, and fears.

Table 2

Selected Strategies for
Evaluation of Effectiveness, Program Initiation

Evaluation Questions	Evaluation Strategies			
	Administrative Audit	Survey	General Accounting	Social Accounting
1. Are there any staff vacancies; how many of the filled positions are a result of recruiting efforts?	X	X		
2. To what extent do community residents perceive the program as related to community needs? To what extent can potential participants be identified; would those persons be willing to participate in the program?	X	X		
3. To what extent is a program plan specified, indicating its objectives and alternative ways to accomplish those objectives?	X			
4. To what extent are budgeting, accounting, and data-collection procedures established in accordance with acceptable practices?			X	X
5. To what extent are personnel policies and practices explicated and consistent with relevant laws and guidelines?	X			
6. To what extent are staff functions and responsibilities delineated?	X			

Note: An "X" indicates that the evaluation strategy in a designated column can be employed to answer the evaluation question in the same row.

The survey approach can be used to obtain additional information for answering Q_1 and Q_2. If there is a large organization with a large staff and administration, a survey of a representative number could be conducted to determine systematically opinions regarding the condi-- tions of their hiring as well as their perceptions of the potential target population. A community-needs survey would provide some estimates about the effectiveness of program planning; the number of potential participants with needs that can be met by the program might be identified, and some indication of the appropriateness of the program could be inferred.

Q_3, Q_5, and Q_6 can be answered adequately by an administrative audit. If a program has a specified plan and has indicated either in staff meetings or written documents that it has alternative approaches in the event of financial contingencies or program-planning failures, it can be inferred that a planning process is in effect. This would be opposite to the finding that the program has no operational plan, which would imply that the administration is deficient in its leadership. Q_5 and Q_6 are directed to important management functions. An auditor can determine whether there are clearly articulated job specifications and personnel policies by reading them and by interviewing staff with respect to their existence and their interpretations. Moreover, those practices and policies would be compared with relevant guidelines to determine the extent to which program management is aware of and in compliance with them.

Q_4 is answered in relation to standards enunciated by accounting and data-processing experts. A standard is a

Table 3

Selected Strategies for
Evaluation of Efficiency, Program Initiation

| | Evaluation Strategies | | |
Evaluation Questions	General Accounting	Administrative Audit	Case Study
1. What are the relative costs of different procedures for the recruitment of staff?	X		
2. In comparison to existing programs of a similar nature, what are the relative costs for the initiation stage of the program?	X		
3. To what extent are staff salaries commensurate with the responsibilities of staff positions, in relation to similar jobs in the community?	X	X	
4. To what extent are there duplicated staff functions that could result in possible ambiguity and conflict?		X	X
5. To what extent do staff persons perceive program objectives as similar or dissimilar; to what extent do staff persons have competing objectives at cross purposes with one another?		X	X
6. To what extent are program activities related to program objectives and/or to program survival?		X	X

Note: An "X" indicates that the evaluation strategy in a designated column can be employed to answer the evaluation question in the same row.

norm of professional practice, which, in the experience of the profession, leads to effective results. For example, a double-entry ledger system may be adjudged by accountants as leading to accurate accountings of finances expended. The accountant reviews the financial accounting system to see whether it contains that procedure or other procedures that will provide accurate financial records. The social accountant (or statistician, or data-processing analyst) also determines whether data-collection procedures are established that lead to reliable and valid information at a minimal cost. Thus, the social accountant attempts to reduce duplication of forms and data-collection devices, while recommending procedures for having a system that can accurately report the number of clients entering and leaving the program, the number and type of services received, and so forth.

EFFICIENCY

General-accounting strategies and procedures can most appropriately be used to answer Q_1 and Q_2. (See table 3.) Assuming that the desired number of persons has been recruited, Q_1 is concerned with which of several possible recruiting procedures is the least costly. For example, a program manager may be interested in whether radio and newspaper advertising is more efficient than door-to-door canvassing and telephone calls. An evaluation would require that cost data be specific for each set of recruiting strategies and that the numbers of successes be recorded in relation to a specified period. With a saturated recruitment effort in which all of the strategies are simultaneously applied to the recruitment of staff, Q_1 could not be answered. An experiment could be employed to provide more definitive information; but the time and costs involved in that strategy would not be worth the effort, unless there are major difficulties in recruiting.

Q_2 may be asked by program sponsors who are interested in comparing the efficiency of similar programs in achieving the requisites for the initiation stage of development. In addition to data on costs per program in relation to projected program size, information must also be gathered about the time it takes for programs to be initiated. Thus, comparisons can be made, but with caution, for they require enough information so factors such as program size and expected difficulties in initiation can be regarded as relatively balanced.

Competing programs may have different salary structures and policies. Efficient management calls for salaries that are competitive for similar responsibilities; hence, Q_3 is aimed at obtaining comparative salary information for similar jobs. A review of job descriptions and salary levels as well as the procurement of data regarding specific staff functions and actual salaries and fringe benefits paid are essential. Hence, the administrative audit is used to supplement accounting data regarding staff payments. An obvious, but often overlooked, result of this evaluation may be that a given program has difficulty in recruiting staff because of comparatively low salaries; a corresponding salary increase may solve the recruiting problem.

Q_4, Q_5, and Q_6 can be answered by means of administrative audits and/or case studies. The intent of Q_4 is to determine whether there appears to be too much duplication and lack of clarity with respect to different staff positions. Certainly there will be tensions or conflict if, for example, equally qualified workers are paid different salaries for identical work. Situations like this could occur with inefficient program planning and management. An administrative audit may review *potential* conflict and ambiguity in job descriptions, but *actual* dissension may not be observable except through interviews and observations of staff performance, which can be obtained through a case study.

The ultimate goals of a social program and the program priorities for achieving immediate objectives should be clear to staff. A program that has personnel who are aware of its objectives and efforts is likely to be relatively efficient. Answers to Q_5 can be obtained by questionnaires and interviews with personnel, as well as through group discussions in one or more staff meetings.

Q_6 distinguishes between program objectives and survival objectives. *Program objectives* refer to those objectives that are devoted to achieving the substance of the program (providing day-care centers, reducing delinquency rates, etc.), and *survival objectives* refer to those that are concerned with keeping a program operational (obtaining necessary funds, providing jobs for program staff, etc.). Obviously, a program must be operational to achieve its substantive goals; but a program concerned only with survival and not with substance may be regarded as inefficient in terms of monies expended for the social welfare of a community. Therefore, information about the relative balance of substantive and survival objectives is important for program sponsors who must decide on the appropriateness of this mix of objectives.

Program Contact

EFFORTS

The time-and-motion study is the primary evaluation strategy that should be used to evaluate the extent of program efforts in the contact stage of development. (See table 4.) Although aspects of survey methodology are employed, we did not include this strategy in table 4 because (1) the survey is not a major evaluation strategy for assessing efforts, and (2) pertinent aspects of survey methodology, such as the formulation of questionnaires, sampling procedures, and modes of data analysis, are incorporated in time-and-motion studies.

Q_1, Q_3, and Q_4 can be answered exclusively by time-and-motion studies. The most important considerations are that the program resources, activities, and contacts are clearly defined and distinguishable, and that the time units of analysis are specified and useable by program staff. The intent of Q_1 is to ascertain the proportion of program time and resources devoted to program contacts. For example, in an evening adult-education program resources might include classrooms, teachers, equipment, textbooks, audio-visual equip-

Table 4
Selected Strategies for Evaluation of Effort, Program Contact

	Evaluation Strategies		
Evaluation Questions	Time-and-Motion Study	Administrative Audit	Social Accounting
1. What amounts of time and program resources are devoted to making program contacts with intended beneficiaries: number of interviews and so on?	X		
2. If a referral system is used, what are the amounts of time and effort involved in referrals?	X		X
3. What efforts are devoted to the compilation of records pertaining to program activity?	X		
4. What amounts of time and activity are devoted to finding resources that could increase the number of program contacts?	X		
5. To what extent are alternative program strategies sought and used, if program efforts do not appear sufficient to reach all of the intended target population?	X	X	

Note: An "X" indicates that the evaluation strategy in a designated column can be employed to answer the evaluation question in the same row.

ment, office supplies, transportation, and so on. The time study would include clear definitions of those resources and the time expended in their use.

The procurement of information regarding Q_3 is necessary for the use of social accounting to evaluate effectiveness in the contact stage. Thus, efforts must be devoted to the selection and formulation of recording devices for appraising the number of program contacts. Without such activities, useful and reliable records could not be established; however, excessive effort would detract from the program's primary function in this stage: to make program contacts.

If additional resources are needed to increase program contacts, it is necessary for the program staff to try to get them. For example, low-income parents may require transportation to attend parent-education meetings. Applicants for a job-training program may need to increase their reading skills before qualifying for the program. Q_4 is concerned with program efforts expended to obtain resources such as transportation and increased reading skills.

Most programs are not able to provide a variety of services that meet all of their clients' needs. But they can refer potential clients to programs that may be more pertinent to their needs, problems, and demands. Program efforts may include the provision of information for referrals, the location of agencies to which clients can be referred, an assessment of need and an informed judgment concerning the most appropriate referrals for specific clients, and so forth. Q_2 refers to the time spent in activities such as these. To compile information about efforts expended in referrals, program contacts must take place, and referrals must be accurately documented and recorded. Although social accounting is a strategy for describing precisely the number of referrals and completions, the time-and-motion study can indicate the proportion of person-hours devoted to referral activities.

If a program's efforts to make contact are unsuccessful, either alternative recruiting strategies are employed or the program is discontinued. Q_4 is asked after there is evidence that a program has not achieved its objectives for the contact stage of development. For example, a health program may have the objective to provide flu shots for a designated target population. As a recruiting strategy, radio broadcasts may not have been successful. Program efforts might be directed to seeking alternative approaches through the literature and interviews with administrators of other programs; it might be found that strategies such as telephone calls and leaflets distributed in schools may be more effective. The administrative audit can provide information of a qualitative nature, that is, whether the program management has sought alternatives and what kinds of efforts took place. If more detailed quantitative information is required, a time-and-motion study could be conducted.

EFFECTIVENESS

It is important to demonstrate in social programs that those actually serviced are representative of the target population. (See table 5.) To be representative, those persons contacted by the program should be similar to

Table 5

Selected Strategies for
Evaluation of Effectiveness, Program Contact

Evaluation Questions	Evaluation Strategies		
	Survey	Social Accounting	Case Study
1. To what extent is the intended target population represented in those who are designated as program beneficiaries?	X	X	
2. What are the opinions of the intended target population regarding the extent to which the content of the program is reaching them and the reasons why program contacts are or are not made?	X		
3. What is the number of appropriate services used, out of the possible number of available referral sources; what are the reasons for the use (or lack of use) of referral services?	X	X	X
4. What happens to prospective clientele who are referred to other programs; how many persons actually receive services from the programs to which they are referred?	X		
5. What is the extent of unsuccessful completions of service or premature terminations, that is, dropouts?		X	

Note: An "X" indicates that the evaluation strategy in a designated column can be employed to answer the evaluation question in the same row.

the target population on eligibility criteria and other characteristics such as race, education level, sex, and social class. For example, if a target population (that population which the program intends to serve) is comprised of 40 per cent Italians, 30 per cent females, and 10 per cent high school graduates, the program beneficiaries should have similar proportions of those groups to be representative. Statistical methods can be employed to determine whether there is a significant discrepancy between the target population and program beneficiaries; a nonstatistically significant discrepancy indicates that the program beneficiaries are representative of the target population.

Information from social-accounting and survey methods can be combined to answer queries about representativeness that are implied in Q_1. Social accounting provides data on the actual number of persons contacted by social programs and their characteristics. If this information is not available in program records, it may be obtained by means of a census of all clientele served or by surveys. Data on characteristics of the target population may also be obtained by means of survey procedures.

Surveys can be employed to provide answers to Q_2 and Q_4. Whereas Q_2 focuses on problems in making initial program contacts, Q_4 is concerned with the extent to which clientele follow through on referrals made to other programs. Representative samples of persons initially contacted by the program and of the clients referred to other programs can be obtained by random sampling, stratified random sampling, and other procedures employed in sample survey methodology. Those groups can then respond to interviews or questionnaires to provide answers to the following kinds of basic questions: why were appointments not kept; were there transportation difficulties; were the clients adequately informed about the program; did they receive similar services elsewhere?

Q_3 is concerned with the referral process. Referrals are often made, but they may be unsuccessful in that clients do not contact the programs to which they are referred or the referrals may be inappropriate. An *inappropriate referral* is one in which the referred program does not have the resources to meet the clients' needs. For example, a client may be referred to a neighborhood service center for financial assistance; it would be inappropriate if that program had no knowledge or resources to provide either financial assistance or access to it. This could lead to feelings of rejection on the part of clients as well as ineffective communication between social programs and agencies. Social accounting can provide information on the actual number of referrals, and surveys of referred persons and the programs to which they are referred can provide data on the extent to which referrals were completed and their appropriateness. If there appears to be a problem in the referral process, more detailed information can be secured through a case-study approach, which might pursue questions as these: what happens in the referral process; how are clients received by different programs; are referrals made even when there are no existing resources; are different social programs cooperating or competing with each other?

Social-accounting procedures are necessary to answer Q_5. Administrators should have records of those who enter, complete, and fail to complete their programs; and those data should be compiled into descriptive statistics. Whereas high completion rates are indicative of effectiveness in the contact stage, high dropout rates may point to possible problems in social planning.

EFFICIENCY

Q_1 is a general question that relies on information concerning effectiveness (i.e., the achievement of program objectives) gathered by other strategies, as well as on the administrative audit and the time-and-motion study. (See table 6.) It essentially deals with the costs of time, manpower, and resources necessary to achieve specified objectives. First, objectives in the contact stage need to be delineated, for example, to provide birth-control information to 90 per cent of a designated population by means of classroom lectures. Second, information concerning the achievement of objectives needs to be gathered, for example, 85 out of 100 were provided with birth-control information. Third, the amount of staff time and other resources to accomplish that objective are obtained through a time-and-motion study, for example, 20 per cent of staff time was employed for that purpose. Then the administrative audit is used to determine major tasks and functions of the program. If, for example, it is shown that the dissemination of birth-control information is *the* major objective of a public-health education program, the administrators of

Table 6

Selected Strategies for
Evaluation of Efficiency, Program Contact

Evaluation Questions	Evaluation Strategies			
	Time-and-Motion Study	Cost Accounting	Administrative Audit	Social Accounting
1. What are the relative proportions of staff time devoted to program objectives, and to what extent is the use of staff time related to the achievement of those objectives?	X		X	
2. What are the relative costs of using different means for contacting clientele?	X	X		
3. Are staff functions and roles structured to maximize program consistency for the achievement of program goals?				X
4. Are certain client characteristics more related to program contact than others; for example, do whites receive more or less program contact than blacks?				X
5. Are certain staff characteristics more related to program contacts than others?				X
6. Are certain staff or client characteristics related to program dropouts?				X

Note: An "X" indicates that the evaluation strategy in a designated column can be employed to answer the evaluation question in the same row.

the program can invest more of their resources in staff time to accomplish their stated objective of dissemination to 90 per cent of the population.

Cost accounting is the basic strategy for answering Q_2. It requires that the methods of establishing program contact are specified and that staff time (and other resources) employed for each method is estimated. For example, during a given month, 20 per cent of staff time may be devoted to door-to-door canvassing that results in contacts with fifty persons; and 5 per cent of staff time may be used in telephone calls that result in contacts with twenty-five persons. If all persons on the staff are equally engaged in the task of making contacts, and if the total staff salary is $10,000, it costs $2,000 to contact fifty persons ($40 per person) by door-to-door canvassing and $500 to contact twenty-five persons ($20 per person) by telephone. Assuming, for illustrative purposes, that other costs, such as transportation and telephone calls, are balanced between the two methods, it can be inferred that the use of telephones is twice as efficient as door-to-door canvassing.

Q_3 can be answered by the administrative audit. The purpose of this question is to determine whether staff are working towards similar goals or are working at cross purposes to one another. Also, the question is concerned with possible unnecessary duplication of functions among various program units and staff persons. Thus, the information produced is concerned primarily with management efficiency in the planning of personnel assignments and in their execution.

The strategy of social accounting (processing and

analyzing statistical data pertinent to staff-client contacts) is used to answer Q_4, Q_5, and Q_6. To answer Q_4 it is first necessary to have a record of the number of program contacts made for a designated group of clients for specified periods. It is also important to have records of client characteristics for the client group, for example, race, sex, and age. Statistical analyses are then employed to determine whether there are any patterns of client characteristics related to program contacts. It might be determined that the proportion of white clients initially contacted in a social program is 10 per cent, but by the third contact, the proportion of whites remaining in the program is 90 per cent. Data such as these can be used to ascertain the possibility of differential selection policies and practices in the processing of clients.

Q_5 is concerned with the relationship of staff characteristics to program contacts. Questions such as these may be pursued: do male workers make more contacts with male or female clients; are younger clients more likely to keep appointments with younger or older workers; are Catholic clients more likely to make appointments with Catholic or non-Catholic workers?

Q_6 is a corollary to Q_4 and Q_5. It is concerned with the extent to which staff and/or client characteristics are related to program dropouts (i.e., failures, in the sense of maintaining contacts). It may be ascertained, for example, that clients of a particular ethnic group will drop out unless they work with staff persons who have the same ethnic identity. In such a program, an administrator may use that information either to match workers and clients by ethnic identity or to inquire further to determine why contacts are not sustained by workers who have different ethnic identities than their clients.

Program Implementation

EFFORTS

In the implementation phase of a program it is administratively desirable to review overall program objectives and activities periodically. This is to ensure that the program has sight of its mission and is not operating mechanistically. (See table 7.) The following five questions (Q_1–Q_5) are focused on the efforts made by administration and staff, and they can be answered basically by means of the administrative audit and time-and-motion studies. Q_1 is concerned with whether there are program reviews by administration and staff. Some programs may have aspirations that are too ambitious and need to consider the extent to which their activities are directly related to those goals. For example, a counseling program for low-income residents may help them to cope with personal problems but still not enable them to escape from poverty. Q_2 is related to Q_1 but is devoted more specifically to the location of additional resources that may help a program achieve its objectives. Sources of referral regarding economic assistance, health insurance, job training, and employment are useful for counseling programs for low-income clientele; efforts should be made to locate those resources.

An important administrative function in the imple-

Table 7
Selected Strategies for
Evaluation of Effort, Program Implementation

Evaluation Questions	Evaluation Strategies	
	Administrative Audit	Time-and-Motion Study
1. How much time and energy are devoted to a review of staff objectives and activities?	X	X
2. What staff efforts are involved in the respecification of goals and in the location of additional resources judged necessary to achieve program results?	X	
3. How much effort is devoted to the specification of criteria for program termination and necessary follow-up activities?	X	
4. How much time and activity are devoted to the procurement of follow-up information from program beneficiaries?		X
5. How much effort is devoted to the consideration and specification of policies for the reentry of dropouts?	X	

Note: An "X" indicates that the evaluation strategy in a designated column can be employed to answer the evaluation question in the same row.

mentation stage is to decide when and under what circumstances recipients should be terminated from the program. What is termination? Can graduates of an education program return to it; are provisions made for continuing education? Are those clients who receive short-term psychotherapy eligible to return for more treatment? These types of questions are implied in Q_3, which is focused on the presence or absence of planning that completes a program cycle.

Many program administrations are ignorant of the postprogram functioning of their clients. Q_4 is focused on the efforts expended by administration and staff to obtain follow-up information. If a job-training program is supposed to train people in specific skills related to particular jobs, follow-up information would indicate the extent to which those persons employed those skills in actual jobs. Without those data the program sponsors and administration would not know whether the program is serving its purpose adequately.

Q_5 is directed at discovering the extent to which administrators have articulated policies regarding the eligibility of dropouts for program reentry. With an unrestricted admission policy and a high turnover rate in program participants, the issue of dropouts may not be problematic. However, in some programs there are waiting lists and eligibility requirements that may affect dropouts. For example, a seventeen-year-old may drop out of a program that has seventeen years of age as an upper limit of eligibility. One month later, he is eighteen years old and wants to return to the program; is he eligible for reentry? Questions like this must be dealt with by administrators who are interested in developing fair and consistent practices for program eligibility.

EFFECTIVENESS

Q_1 is a basic question regarding the effectiveness of social programs that have been fully implemented. (See table 8.) It is asking about results (or outcomes) that are correlated with programs. Moreover, it specifies general areas in which results might occur: knowledge, attitudes, skills, behaviors. Obviously, Q_1 must be specified further in relation to the particular program that is being evaluated. For example, a program may have the objectives of teaching basic English and facts about the United States Constitution to recent Italian immigrants. A knowledge test may be devised to reflect comprehension of English, and a skills test may reflect the extent to which persons are capable of writing business and personal letters; an objective, multiple-choice test may be constructed to represent knowledge of the Constitution. Q_1, then, is transformed into this question: to what extent have increases in knowledge (regarding English comprehension and understanding of the Constitution) and skills (regarding the ability to write letters) occurred as a function of the program? This question may be answered by means of experiments or surveys. An interrupted time-series design (see Epstein and Tripodi, *Research Techniques for Program Planning, Monitoring and Evaluation*), a quasi-experimental design, may be employed in which repeated measures of knowledge and skill are taken before and subsequent to the initiation of

Table 8

Selected Strategies for
Evaluation of Effectiveness, Program Implementation

Evaluation Questions	Evaluation Strategies	
	Experiment	Survey
1. What results have been achieved that could be attributed to the program; are there discernible changes in the knowledge, attitudes, or skills of the program beneficiaries; are there changes in behavior on the part of individuals, groups, or organizations?	X	X
2. What results could have been obtained without the content of the program (would changes have taken place anyway)?	X	
3. Are there any unplanned outcomes, either desirable or undesirable, that could be attributed to the program?	X	X
4. How effective is the program in relation to the need of the intended target population?	X	X

Note: An "X" indicates that the evaluation strategy in a designated column can be employed to answer the evaluation question in the same row.

the program to determine the extent of change. Surveys may be taken of persons who have completed the program, are in the program, and are waiting to enter the program; from those surveys estimates of change can be made. However, neither of those approaches provides sufficient evidence concerning causality, which is the essence of Q_2. Such data may be obtained by the use of experimental and control groups in a classical experimental design. For example, Italian immigrants are randomly assigned to either an experimental group or a control group. Persons in both groups are given tests of knowledge and skill; then those assigned to the experimental group receive an educational program, and those in the control group receive no program. After a specified period of time, persons in both groups are given the tests again. If significant increases in knowledge and skill are observed for the experimental group, and not for the control group, inferences can be made regarding the program's influence on changes in knowledge and skill.

Q_3 requires that evaluators and administrators look beyond goal achievement and consider whether there are other outcomes, or side effects, of a program that may be either helpful or harmful to program beneficiaries. A new drug may lead to the achievement of an objective to reduce headaches, but it may also lead to malfunctioning kidneys. On the other hand, an educational program for low-income delinquent youth may accomplish its objective of enabling the youth to receive high school diplomas and may also lead to more jobs and less delinquent activity, which is a desirable side effect of the educational program. Such side effects can be observed in the context of experiments and surveys, as long as evaluators are prepared to anticipate and measure program consequences other than the achievement of program objectives.

Q_4 also intends to look at the effectiveness of a program from a broader perspective. Its aim is to provide data on comprehensiveness, the ratio of effectiveness to community need. Effectiveness can be most easily determined by experiments, and needs can be ascertained by survey (or epidemiological) procedures. A dental-hygiene program may have the objective of reducing the number of cavities in low-income persons enrolled in the program. It may be effective in that each of ten persons enrolled in the program had the number of cavities reduced to zero; however, the program may not be very comprehensive because a survey indicates that there are over 2,000 low-income persons in that community who need such a program. The survey may have been an estimate, based on a representative sample of the low-income population. Persons in the sample may have been examined by dentists to indicate whether they had cavities, and they may have been queried about whether they were planning to seek dental treatment. Those persons with cavities but who were not planning to seek dental treatment might have been regarded as in "need" of the dental-hygiene program.

EFFICIENCY

Cost-analytic strategies and research methods are the primary approaches for answering evaluation questions of efficiency in the implementation stage. (See table 9.) General accounting and cost-effectiveness, supplemented by experimental knowledge, are the most frequently employed approaches.

Q_1 is a question that leads to a special type of cost-effectiveness study. Within the framework of an experiment comparing the relative effectiveness of two or more techniques, general-accounting procedures are employed to obtain information regarding the actual expenditures for each technique; moreover, with a demonstration of equivalent degrees of effectiveness for each technique, cost-effectiveness methodology can be employed to gauge the relative efficiency of each technique. To illustrate: a counseling program may have several strategies for achieving results: (a) individual counseling; (b) group counseling; and (c) combinations of group and individual counseling. General-accounting procedures may indicate that more manpower and program resources (hence, greater expenditures) are

Table 9

Selected Strategies for
Evaluation of Efficiency, Program Implementation

Evaluation Questions	Evaluation Strategies			
	General Accounting	Experiment	Cost Effectiveness	Cost Benefit
1. What are the relative costs of different techniques used to achieve similar results?	X	X	X	
2. What is the relation of costs of program effort to the benefits of results achieved?	X			X
3. What are the relative costs of the program in comparison with other programs with similar objectives?	X	X	X	
4. Could the same results be achieved with a reduction in program efforts?		X	X	

Note: An "X" indicates that the evaluation strategy in a designated column can be employed to answer the evaluation question in the same row.

allocated to c than to b, and to b as opposed to a. An experiment may be conducted in which persons with similar counseling needs, the reduction of anxiety, are assigned randomly to one of three experimental groups in which counselors may employ a, b, or c. An analysis of anxiety measures before and after the strategies are implemented indicates that there are no statistically significant differences among the experimental groups. Hence, a is most efficient, and technique c is the least efficient.

Q_2 directly leads to cost-benefit analysis. Relying on previous information of effectiveness through experiments or approximation to experiments and surveys, the cost-benefit analyst seeks data regarding the expenditures on program efforts. He or she then seeks to translate the data on effectiveness into "benefits," that is, a measure of dollars and cents. Ratios of benefits to costs of program efforts are subsequently produced. The greater the benefits per cost, the more efficient is the program. The societal benefits from a job-training program may include items such as the money earned in subsequent employment and monies contributed to local, state, and federal governments through taxes; the costs may refer to the monies expended for rental, supplies, salaries for staff, and so on.

Q_3 is a question leading to comparisons of similar programs. The strategies employed to answer it are identical to those employed for Q_1; however, it is much more difficult, because of the greater degrees of complexity and lack of control in comparing programs as contrasted with techniques within a program. Thus, many more assumptions are made, and the conclusions are less definite. Nevertheless, the data are useful to program sponsors, social planners, and policy analysts.

Q_4 is intended to lead to an experimental manipulation that reduces program efforts. For example, a public-health program to stop smoking may have used twenty hours of staff time to decrease the amount of cigarettes smoked (from twenty-five to zero per day) for each program beneficiary. An experiment could be employed to compare the twenty hours of staff time with a reduced amount of staff time, for example, ten hours. If the same results are achieved with either ten or twenty hours of staff time, the inference can be made that a reduction in staff time is relatively efficient.

BIBLIOGRAPHY

Babbie, Earl R. *Survey Research Methods,* pp. 73–129. Belmont, Calif.: Wadsworth Publishing Company, 1973.

Epstein, Irwin, and Tripodi, Tony. *Research Techniques for Program Planning, Monitoring and Evaluation,* chapters 2, 3, 6, 7, and 12. New York: Columbia University Press, 1977.

Epstein, Irwin; Tripodi, Tony; and Fellin, Phillip. "Community Development Programs and Their Evaluation." In *Social Workers at Work.* 2nd ed., pp. 182–92. Edited by Tony Tripodi, Phillip Fellin, Irwin Epstein, and Roger Lind. Itasca, Ill.: F. E. Peacock Publishers, 1977.

Levin, Henry M. "Cost-Effectiveness Analysis in

Evaluation Research." In *Handbook of Evaluation Research*. Vol. 2, pp. 89–122. Edited by Marcia Guttentag and Elmer L. Struening. Beverly Hills, Calif.: Sage Publications, 1975.

Livingstone, John L., and Gunn, Sanford C. *Accounting for Social Goals*, pp. 35–38, 117–70, and 313–54. New York: Harper and Row, 1974.

Suchman, Edward A. *Evaluation Research*, chapters 3 and 4. New York: Russell Sage Foundation, 1967.

Terry, George R. *Principles of Management*. 6th ed., chapters 1, 3, 10, and 22–26. Homewood, Ill.: Richard D. Irwin, 1972.

Chapter Six

USE OF CONSULTATION

Throughout this book we have emphasized the key role the program director plays in the planning of social program evaluations. Thus, we have presented guidelines that can be helpful to the administrator in thinking about differential evaluation. Since program directors are not likely to be expert in conducting most types of evaluations, it is important now to consider ways in which evaluation consultants can be used.

There are at least two phases of evaluation planning in which the administrator may wish to use evaluation consultants. In the first instance, the director may seek consultation to assist in deciding whether a program should be evaluated. In considering this question, the program director must take into account dilemmas connected with the potential costs of evaluation, the people and purposes for which the evaluation will be conducted, and the choice of a program evaluator.

With a review of the preceding chapters, and trusting their own competence and knowledge of evaluation techniques, some administrators will be in a position to decide, on their own, whether to evaluate. However, evaluation consultants can be of help to many administrators who lack experience and knowledge about evaluation or who seek to legitimize evaluation efforts. Once the program director has decided to proceed with an evaluation, he or she is faced with two choices: (1) The director and his or her staff may conduct the evaluation themselves (see Epstein and Tripodi); or (2) they may choose an evaluator to do it. This second choice, the task of choosing an evaluator, is the focus of this chapter.

PROGRAM EVALUATION OR NOT

Administrators are often confronted with the decision of whether a program should be evaluated. There are several factors that should be considered in making this decision, and, after the program director's initial examination of these, he or she may wish to make use of an evaluation consultant. One of the potential advantages in using a consultant is the probability that consultation will provide a clear, informed foundation for later negotiations with an evaluator, if it is decided to carry out an evaluation effort.

The first task of the program director in evaluation planning is to state with clarity the program's objectives.[1]

---

[1] Edward Suchman (see Bibliography) has specified a number of criteria for delineating program objectives. Those criteria can be summarized by these

If the program goals are not specified, it will be unclear what is to be evaluated. Obviously, evaluations cannot provide feedback information regarding the accomplishment of goals when the goals are unknown. Second, the degree of certainty of knowledge about the program should be considered. If the director, for example, knows that his or her program (and programs similar to it) are effective and efficient in achieving program goals, there may be little need for an evaluation. On the other hand, there may be insufficient evidence that the program is working; in fact, the administrator may not even know what activities are specifically taking place in the program. Third, the possibility of change in program goals should be considered. A program in the process of development must have feedback information regarding its goals—its successes and failures. Fourth, one should weigh the relative advantages and disadvantages of evaluation. What kinds of information can be secured from evaluation, and could that information be used for the continuing development of the program?

Previously, we presented the notion of evaluation for different stages of program development as a conceptual device for clarifying the kinds of questions one would want answered in an evaluation. If one assumes that a program is in one stage of development, and asks questions not appropriate for that stage, the evaluation is

---

questions: *Who* (what staff persons?) does *what* (what is the program technology?) to *whom* (what are characteristics of the population the program intends to serve?), *where* (in what locations?), for *what duration* of time (over what period is the program technology to be employed?), and with *what expected changes* (are there expected changes in knowledge, attitudes, skills, or behavior; what is the magnitude of expected change; when will the changes occur?)?

not likely to provide information that can be used by program administration. Thus, the process of forming differential evaluation questions is a way of considering whether evaluation might be advantageous. Moreover, it is a device for determining the timing of different kinds of evaluation. Evaluations devoted to an assessment of the implementation stage, for example, are not likely to provide useful information to the administrator for making program decisions when his or her program plan is just being conceived in the program-initiation stage. That is, an evaluation of the implementation stage in this instance would be premature.

The following questions are presented as preliminary guidelines for the administrator who is considering a differential evaluation of a social program:

1. What is the current state of program objectives?
   a. What are current program objectives?
   b. Are the program objectives likely to change?
   c. What is the current state of knowledge of the program?
2. What is the purpose of the evaluation?
   a. What stage of development is to be evaluated?
   b. What are the relative advantages and disadvantages of an evaluation?
   c. Would the program be altered as a result of feedback from the evaluation?

These guidelines point to minimal sets of information necessary for the program administrator's decision on the question of whether a program should be evaluated. It is particularly important for the program director to accept major responsibility for ascertaining this information, and he or she should not expect this task to be performed by an evaluation consultant. However, an evaluation consultant may be of considerable assistance in reviewing the stated objectives of a program and checking on their clarity and specificity before a final decision to evaluate or not.

EVALUATION AT WHAT COST

A major issue that confronts administrators planning evaluation is the cost of an evaluation. What funds are available for an evaluation? What kinds of information can be obtained from evaluations that are limited in their comprehensiveness by the amounts and types of resources available? Essentially, the primary question is: what are the administrative costs of evaluation in relation to the potential value of an evaluation?

There are two major kinds of costs: primary costs and secondary costs. *Primary costs* are all of the direct costs involved in the procurement of evaluation manpower, time, physical resources, and operational facilities for the conduct of an evaluation. How much money is available to pay evaluation consultants, to provide facilities for the compilation of necessary evaluation data, and so forth? *Secondary costs* are those indirect costs that occur when an evaluation is planned and when it is actually executed. That is, secondary costs are concerned with the effects of the evaluation effort on program operations and the commitments of time, effort, and program resources required to facilitate the evaluation.

A program director should be knowledgeable about the secondary costs as well as the primary costs of evaluation. The reason for this is that program resources used for purposes of an evaluation may detract from the manpower and time necessary for the program staff to carry out its program. While an evaluation is taking place, it is possible that some program costs might be reduced. For example, immediate procedures for the efficient allocation of program resources may be developed. Moreover, it is possible that a program may receive direct financial benefits from an evaluation. This may occur when an evaluation is funded entirely through other sources (e.g., grants for demonstration projects from governmental and private foundations), and part of the evaluation monies are used to subsidize some program costs, such as selected clerical activities.

In summary, the answers to the following questions should be considered by the administrator who is planning an evaluation:

1. What funds from the program and other resources are available for evaluation?
2. What are the primary costs of a proposed evaluation?
3. What are the secondary costs of a projected evaluation?
4. What are the potential benefits of an evaluation?

The extent to which administrators will be able to

ascertain the answers to these questions without assistance will depend upon several factors, such as the technical competencies of the administrator and staff members, the particular stage of program development, and the kinds of evaluation techniques appropriate to the evaluation. Thus, many administrators will need to use an evaluation consultant when complex evaluation designs, such as experiments, are contemplated at the implementation stage of a program. Evaluation consultants will be of particular help in estimating primary costs of evaluation. The administrator should not hesitate to use an evaluation consultant with regard to cost estimates, for neglect in this area will likely lead to unanticipated conflict, during an evaluation, between the administrator and evaluator. Since costs are so closely interconnected with the choice of evaluation techniques, evaluation consultants competent in the various techniques are ready sources for cost-related planning.

EVALUATION FOR WHOM

In planning for evaluation, the administrator must ask: who is the consumer of evaluation? Different groups who are the consumers of evaluation may have diverse values and discrepant notions of what the program goals and evaluation should be. For example, a group that has fiduciary responsibility for a program may be most concerned about the potential mismanagement of funds and program efficiency; and a group that is representative of the target population may be most interested in the extent to which the program services are meeting their most pressing community needs. What is an acceptable evaluation for one group of consumers may not be acceptable to another group. In particular, criteria for acceptable evaluations may differ for consumers who have vested interest in the maintenance of a program, as opposed to consumers who are in competition with the program.

In our view, then, it would be unrealistic for an administrator to assume that all consumers of evaluation have equivalent values and to ignore the sociopolitical context in which an evaluation might take place. Thus, no single evaluation can serve all consumers in the same way. Even if all groups of potential consumers are known before an evaluation, it may be impossible for those groups to agree on program objectives and the criteria for assessing them. Therefore, in the planning of an evaluation, the administrator should consider the following factors:

1. Is the sociopolitical climate conducive to an evaluation (see chapter 1)?
2. Who are the potential consumers of evaluation?
3. To what groups is the program most accountable; are their priorities regarding program goals and content similar to those of the program staff and administration?
4. Are there other groups that have vested interests in the success of the program and competing groups with vested interests in the failure of the program?

5. Is there any existing controversy regarding any aspect of the program?

6. To what extent is it possible to solicit the involvement of the above groups in clarifying objectives and criteria for evaluating program goals at different stages of development?

The answers to these questions have implications for the kind of evaluation the program director undertakes and for the choice of an evaluator. In some sociopolitical contexts, even the carrying out of a survey may be problematic. Also, the status and reputation of an evaluator may be sufficiently influential to allow for such an evaluation. Information about the potential consumers of evaluation constitutes an essential part of the discussions between the program director and a prospective program evaluator, as conditions and expectations under which an evaluation can be undertaken are identified.

EVALUATION BY WHOM

Given a decision to evaluate a program, the administrator is concerned with questions such as these: who should conduct the program evaluation; who has the necessary competence; and who is available and willing to do an evaluation? Perhaps the director's first consideration is whether he or one of his staff members can conduct the evaluation, and, if so, is outside consultation needed? In this regard, the administrator needs to be alert to the potential advantages and disadvantages in the use of "inside" versus "outside" program evaluators. The traditional argument for the use of an outside evaluator is that he or she can be more objective, because of a lack of involvement in the organizational system. In addition, the outside evaluator is assumed to be more likely accepted as an expert by the staff and consumers of an evaluation. Since the outside evaluator is not a part of the authority structure of the organization, he or she is expected to be in a preferred position for giving advice and for making recommendations that will be less threatening to the administrator and his or her staff. On the negative side, the outside evaluator is normally unknown to the program staff and, therefore, more likely to be a source of anxiety to them and to cause a certain amount of disequilibrium within the organization. Of course, the program director is often able to take steps to minimize these problems through appropriate briefing of staff for the evaluation.

Perhaps the principal advantage of the inside evaluator, who comes from within the organization, is that he or she is less likely to have entry problems, such as the need to learn about the program objectives and operations, and will be accepted by the staff. The inside evaluator is assumed to have the advantage of knowing the staff and to be able to carry out an evaluation without upsetting the operations of the program. In addition, it is assumed that the inside evaluator will have values regarding program goals and evaluation objectives consistent with those of the administrator. However, the insider's evaluation may be suspect to some, as not being completely objective and as providing biased findings. Another concern regarding the inside evaluator is that his or her other organizational roles may present demands that inhibit the conduct of the evaluation and prevent or delay its completion. Finally, although it is generally thought that the inside consultant is less costly than the outside person, this is not necessarily the case, particularly when secondary costs are taken into account.

How does a program director solve this dilemma between the use of inside and outside evaluation consultants and evaluators? By taking our view of differential evaluation, the program director will at times require an outside evaluator, or an inside evaluator, or both. Thus, for some stages of program development, the limitations cited with regard to the use of inside evaluators may be minimal or be easily overcome. At other stages, such as evaluation at the implementation stage of a program, the advantage of an outside evaluator may be most salient. The program director should carefully examine the evaluation needs of the program and seek out evaluators at specific stages of development with inside-outside evaluation issues in mind. If appropriate persons are not available and/or desirable from within the organizational system, the administrator may use an evaluation consultant to assist in selecting an evaluator from outside the system. In some cases, such a consultant will stay on to be the program evaluator, or he or she may simply assist the administrator in finding an evaluator.

As the program director considers who the evaluator should be, the administrative and technical roles defined for the evaluator must also be taken into account. In general, the evaluator's role may be defined in terms of providing for systematic feedback of information regarding evaluation objectives. In addition, it must be clear whether the evaluator is to participate in helping to implement evaluation findings. For example, an administrator may be interested in having an evaluator solve specific problems, obtain specific information, make a report, and depart. Or he or she may expect the evaluator also to assist in handling possible resistance of staff to evaluation and to change, to assist in developing skills for solving organizational problems, or to carry out recommendations. In such instances, the program director will seek an evaluator who has certain skills in social relationships and/or training in this area. As the program director defines the evaluator's role, he or she will then be wise to weigh the relative advantages and disadvantages of evaluators from inside as compared to outside the organization. Thus, when the evaluator's role includes considerable activity in implementing findings directed toward organizational change, the administrator may prefer an inside evaluator.

The administrator must also consider the manner in which an evaluation consultant will be expected to relate to the organization's administrative structure. For example, in some cases the administrator may want to retain complete jurisdiction over his or her own program staff and the evaluation staff; in other instances, the program director and evaluator may share administrative authority or work out an agreement of division of responsibility. A characteristic frequently attributed to evaluators is the inability of the administrator to control the behaviors of the evaluation team. This is particularly relevant in the light of the "authoritative" nature of the image of the evaluator. Clearly spelled out administrative relationships become an important prerequisite for sound evaluations and serve to add predictability to the evaluator's performance. Thus, the role of the evaluator, with appropriate attention to issues regarding inside-outside evaluations, must be carefully thought out as the program director proceeds to select someone to evaluate his or her program.

Expertise of the Consultant

The selection of an evaluator must, in large part, be based on the expertise required for a particular program evaluation. As we indicated in chapter 4, most evaluators are not likely to be expert in all evaluation strategies, and different evaluation consultants may differ in their methodological preferences. Thus, one evaluator may emphasize cost-accounting methods, and another may emphasize experimental methods.

In addition to the preference for selected strategies, evaluators may differ in their conceptions of the kinds of knowledge that should be derived from evaluations. Evaluation of a program can be viewed as a field situation in which new insights and hypotheses will be developed for the refinement of theory. Such information might be useful to the evaluator who is a theoretician, but it may not be practicable for the program staff. An alternative conception is that an evaluation can provide facts and verified hypotheses pertinent to the specific program being evaluated. In this instance, the evaluator's role may be similar to that of the engineer: he or she devises and executes an evaluation design to test program hypotheses.

The implication for the administrator who is planning an evaluation is that he or she should be knowledgeable about what kind of evaluation is desired for what stage of program development. Moreover, the administrator should be aware of the possibility that different evaluators may emphasize different values with regard to evaluation.

An evaluator may be in agreement with program goals, and he or she may view evaluation as a strategy to force the program staff to operate in desired ways. Such an evaluator may be a social reformer who is more interested in program development than in providing information regarding the achievement of program goals. Alternatively, another evaluator may view social programs as essentially wasteful. He or she may believe that rigorous evaluations usually lead to no significant differences as a result of program efforts, and it is possible that he or she might sacrifice program substance for inappropriate experimental designs.

An important aspect of the consultant's credentials will be his or her professional discipline. This partially defines the perspective the individual is likely to take toward evaluation. An important question for the administrator is the extent to which he or she needs an evaluator who has knowledge of the social-practice problems related to the evaluation. Thus, in many cases, maximum benefit comes from an evaluation consultant who is from a discipline other than that of the administrator.

In summary, before an evaluation, the administrator should ascertain the specific technical expertise of the prospective evaluator, as well as his or her conceptual, methodological, and value biases. He or she should then correlate that information with his or her knowledge of what kind of evaluation is most appropriate to the problem at hand and the potential consumers of the evaluation. The following questions pertaining to the selection of an evaluator are presented as factors that should be considered in planning an evaluation:

1. What is the technical competency of the evaluator?
2. Are technically competent evaluators available?
3. What is the evaluator's conception of evaluation?
4. Does the evaluator have a strong bias in favor of or opposed to the content of the program?
5. Does the evaluator have a vested interest in the program or in competing programs?

The task for the administrator is to select the most pertinent expert for evaluation purposes. Answering the above questions will assist the administrator in making an appropriate selection. Of particular help will be at least an elementary knowledge of evaluation strategies, such as monitoring, social-research, and cost-analytic procedures. Our review of these strategies in chapter 4 and our specification of differential evaluation in chapter 5 provide a foundation for linking evaluation needs to technical evaluation approaches and hence to evaluation experts.

Sources of Evaluation Consultants

There are a number of sources to which the program director may look for evaluation consultants. Within large organizations, the program director may turn to other units, such as research, budgeting, and statistics. In seeking an outside evaluator, the administrator may seek out experts from organizations with programs similar to his or look to members of professional organizations. A variety of kinds of experts can be found in university settings and in independent contracting organizations, such as survey research centers, private business organizations, and consulting firms.

Perhaps the single most relevant contingency regarding the selection of program evaluators is the availability of funds. Since funds are always to some extent limited, the administrator must search for experts within the context of available money. When funds are extremely scarce, the administrator may look to individuals within the organization who have some expertise in evaluation and who can be reassigned to such tasks. Or, under these circumstances, the administrator may search for a consultant (from within or without the organization) who will devote his or her efforts to seeking funds for evaluation.

Although knowledge of these sources is important for finding an appropriate consultant or evaluator, the administrator must also recognize the implications of the expert's organizational ties for the conduct of the evaluation and use of findings. As we have pointed out, when the evaluator comes from within the organization there may be some advantages, such as his or her more complete knowledge of the program, immediate access to the administrator, minimized entry problems, and commitment to evaluation objectives. Particular attention must also be given to the administrative arrangements, so it is clear whether the evaluator's position is advisory to or subordinate to the administrator's. Thus, the administrator should be aware of the potential uses and abuses of consultants and evaluators that accrue from the organizational and administrative context in which they are placed.

Exploratory Interviews

When the program administrator has decided on the need for an evaluation and has located a potential evaluator, he or she should proceed to an interview with the individual for an exchange of ideas. As indicated earlier, the administrator has the responsibility for providing the prospective evaluator with information about the program, evaluation objectives, and so on. This information serves as a principal basis to the administrator and evaluator for deciding whether the evaluation can answer questions regarding program objectives and can be undertaken with available staff and resources.

In our earlier discussion of the expertise of evaluators,

we identified several guideline questions to assist the administrator in ascertaining the suitability of an evaluator for a specific evaluation effort. During the exploratory interview, therefore, the administrator is interested in the "goodness of fit" between the evaluator and program objectives, staff, and organizational values. Thus, the administrator wants to learn whether the consultant is sensitive to the values of the organization and the extent to which the consultant's values are congruent with those of the organization. In addition, the administrator wants to discover the evaluator's overall conception of evaluation and something about his methodological competence, as well as his or her understanding of the program to be evaluated. The administrator will want to determine whether the evaluator's expertise is relevant to the evaluation task.

During the initial interview(s), the administrator should explore ideas concerning the role relationships of the evaluator to the administration and staff. He or she will want to make some preliminary assessment of how the evaluator's role will complement the roles of program staff. He or she should begin to clarify the role of the evaluator and to formulate ways in which the evaluator will use his or her own staff and that of the organization to carry out the evaluation. Discussion should also focus on the time deemed necessary for an evaluation, the time investment required by the evaluator and by the administrator and staff, the costs of employment of the evaluator and his or her assistants, and the possible use of additional consultants and their relationships to the evaluator.

In the exploratory interviews, the evaluator has the opportunity to learn about the program and evaluation objectives and to decide whether he or she is interested in the evaluation and wishes to work with the program director. The administrator also wants to work with someone who is competent and who can produce information relevant to the program. He or she therefore makes this assessment during the initial interviews and determines how well he or she and the evaluator relate to each other. The administrator seeks out areas that might cause conflict and that could impede the evaluation efforts, rather than assuming that the evaluation task is solely the responsibility of the evaluator.

ESTABLISHING THE CONTRACT

Perhaps one of the best ways to facilitate the evaluation effort is to establish a contract with the evaluator. The contract should spell out the mutually agreed-upon commitments and obligations of the administrator and the evaluator. Included in the contract should be a clear statement of role expectations, commitments of time and personnel, funding commitments, administrative juris- dictions, and proposed use of findings. Since decisions cannot all be made in the planning stage of an evaluation effort, a plan should be made for handling decisions on emerging issues, as well as for the possible renegotiation of the contract at specified dates. An important commitment concerns the type of involvement the administrator and his or her staff will have in the evaluation process. Both the administrator and the evaluator need a clear understanding in advance of the various alternatives for use of staff and of the restrictions placed in the evaluator's use of staff. To illustrate, an evaluation consultant might rely on written records and/or receipt of information from recipients of service, while not using or contacting staff members. Another model might involve the staff member's involvement in data-collection efforts, rating, coding of information, and so forth. In still another model, the staff member may himself be a subject of the evaluation effort, contributing to the evaluation by completing forms, interviews, and so on. The essential element here is the specification of the ways in which the evaluator will use and/or study various staff members, so potential conflicts can be identified and handled. These are particularly important concerns, since they involve staff time and program resources.

Since the purpose of the evaluation is frequently an assessment that will contribute to change and improvement, the role of the evaluator with regard to use of findings must be specified. For example, it must be clear whether the evaluator is expected only to make recommendations for change, or also to help bring change about through interpretation of findings, training efforts, and the like.

Based on our review of the various stages of program development, the administrator must negotiate with the evaluator with regard to his or her relationship to one or more program stages. In some cases, movement from one program stage to another (e.g., from program initiation to program contact) will call for a change in program-evaluation expertise. In other cases, there will be advantages in continuing with the same evaluator. The mechanisms for making these decisions should be specified in the initial contract with the evaluator. The administrator will also want to specify times at which he or she will evaluate the contribution of the evaluator and when decisions are to be made regarding continuation of employment.

THE EVALUATION PHASE

Although the contract between the administrator and the evaluator provides a basis for activities during the evaluation period, there are a number of additional issues the administrator must resolve. The administrator will want to work with the evaluator to avoid undue resistance to evaluation by staff members and to create realistic expectations on their part. He or she will want to be alert to entry problems the evaluator may have, as well as to problems that may come from some staff members becoming overdependent on the evaluator because he or she is seen as an oracle of "great authority."

As the evaluation proceeds, the administrator will want to develop further plans with the evaluator for the report of findings, that is, feedback mechanisms that will facilitate the consideration and use of findings. With this in mind, the administrator must attend to the positive aspects of staff involvement and communication regarding the use of evaluation. Although the evaluator is a key person in interpreting the results of an evaluation through reports and personal communication, actual change will likely depend upon behaviors of the administrator and staff. The administrator should work with the evaluator throughout the evaluation period, to the extent necessary to reach evaluation objectives and to allow for program change when indicated. The role of the evaluator at the termination phase of an evaluation is of particular concern to the administrator. Under most conditions, the evaluator is not expected to continue with the program indefinitely, and the administrator must anticipate and plan for his or her departure. Some of the functions performed by the evaluator may well be taken over by the administrator and/or his or her staff members.

USE OF FINDINGS

At the completion of an evaluation, the program director is faced with the task of using the evaluation results for making programmatic decisions. Evaluation consultants can be called upon to assist in answering questions such as the following:

1. What do the findings mean in terms of the program objectives?
2. How can the findings be used to bring about changes in a particular program?
3. What implications would the implementation of findings have for the overall program?
4. What next steps are necessary, such as new evaluation efforts, implementation of change, or movement to new stages of program development?

The program director may want to rely heavily on the program evaluator for consideration of these questions, or he or she may wish to include additional consultants in these deliberations. The need for consultation at this point will vary, depending on factors such as the nature of the evaluation objectives, the kinds of knowledge gained from the evaluation, and the type of implementation possible and desirable. Since the evaluation results will deal with the efforts, effectiveness, and efficiency of social programs, the program director will want to consider implementation with regard to information received about these aspects of the program operations. For each of these areas, the director will be concerned with the soundness, or validity, of the knowledge obtained and the extent to which it reduces uncertainty about achievements of program objectives. The evaluator will be a key person in interpreting the meaning of the evaluation findings to the administrator and his or her staff. In those cases when the administrator must report the evaluation results to outside groups, such as boards of directors, it is essential that he or she capitalize on the expertise of the evaluator, as well as on other available consultants, to assess the implications of the findings.

Following the assessment of the soundness of the evaluation results, the administrator must make decisions regarding what findings can be put into actual program practice. He or she is concerned here with engineerability of the new knowledge, that is, the extent to which the variables under study are available for control by program personnel, and whether the manipulation of the variables is feasible. For example, a variable such as the administrator's control over the budget of his or her program may have a high degree of manipulability. However, even though highly manipulable, the budget changes would then be evaluated in terms of the strength of their effect on the desired program change and the feasibility of such activity. Thus, the economic costs of other programs in an organization, and other organizational constraints, would then have to be considered in deciding whether to manipulate the budget.

It is at this point, with the evaluation findings in, that the usefulness of the results must be assessed and that evaluation efforts take on their full meaning, that is, as a management technique for the administrator of social programs. Evaluation consultants, of course, are key resource persons in regard to the administrator's decisions, but, in the final analysis, the program administrator must take the primary responsibility for the evaluation and the subsequent use of the information. Hence, for the administrator, the evaluation provides a foundation for making decisions about the program, based on available, objective information that can be used to provide effective and efficient program services in health, education, and welfare.

BIBLIOGRAPHY

Davis, Howard R., and Salasin, Susan E. "The Utilization of Evaluation." In *Handbook of Evaluation Research*. Vol. 1, pp. 621–66. Edited by Elmer L. Struening and Marcia Guttentag. Beverly Hills, Calif.: Sage Publications, 1975.

Epstein, Irwin, and Tripodi, Tony. *Research Techniques for Program Planning, Monitoring and Evaluation,* pp. 29–41. New York: Columbia University Press, 1977.

Suchman, Edward A. *Evaluative Research,* pp. 51–73 and 151–68. New York: Russell Sage Foundation, 1967.

Tripodi, Tony. *Uses and Abuses of Social Research in Social Work,* pp. 175–97. New York: Columbia University Press, 1974.

Weiss, Carol H. *Evaluation Research,* pp. 110–28. Englewood Cliffs, N.J.: Prentice-Hall, 1972.

INDEX

THE BOOK MANUFACTURE

Differential Social Program Evaluation was composed, printed and bound at The Parthenon Press, Nashville, Tennessee. Cover design was by Martin Alt. The type is Caledonia with Lisbon display.